The
Developing
Child

Fathers

Fathers

Ross D. Parke

Harvard University Press
Cambridge, Massachusetts

To my mother
and father

Copyright © 1981 by Ross D. Parke
All rights reserved
Printed in the United States of America
10 9 8 7 6 5 4 3
Library of Congress Cataloging in Publication Data
   Parke, Ross D
      Fathers.

      (The Developing child)
      Bibliography: p.
      1. Fathers. 2. Father and child. 3. Child
development. I. Title. II. Series: Developing
child.
HQ756.P38   306.8'7   80-29079
ISBN 0-674-29515-3
ISBN 0-674-29516-1 (pbk.)

Acknowledgments

My own research reported in this volume has been supported by grants from a variety of agencies over the last decade: The Grant Foundation; the National Foundation March of Dimes; The National Institute of Child Health and Human Development; the Graduate School of the University of Illinois; and the Fels Fund of Philadelphia. A number of persons have contributed in important ways to the research program at the University of Wisconsin, the Fels Research Institute, the University of Cincinnati College of Medicine, and most recently the University of Illinois. Sandra O'Leary was an important early collaborator. Douglas Sawin, my friend and co-worker at Fels and Cincinnati, gave wisdom, effort, and moral support. At Illinois, Thomas Power and Barbara Tinsley have been active in our research on fathers. Steve Asher made helpful comments on early chapters of this book, and Graeme Russell provided useful material and insights for the final chapter. Special thanks to Barbara Tinsley for encouragement and detailed feedback at all stages of the writing. The book was completed when I was a visiting Research Scholar at Macquarie University in Australia; I am grateful to Jacqueline Goodnow for the opportunity to visit and work there. Eric Wanner was generous with encouragement and editorial guidance, and Camille Smith edited the final draft with skill. Elaine Babb deserves a special appreciation for tracking down numerous obscure statistics and references, and Brenda Congdon and Eileen Posluszny did a fine job of preparing the manuscript. Thanks, too, to my wife, Sue, and my children, Gillian, Timothy, and Megan, for their support and advice during the writing of the book. Finally, I want to express my thanks to other father researchers and to the many families who have consented to be studied to help us learn about fathers and fathering.

Contents

1 / Fatherhood: Myths and Realities

A famous anthropologist once said that fathers are a biological necessity, but a social accident. Throughout much of the present century and all of the last, our culture has conformed comfortably to this view. Traditionally, fathers have been portrayed as uninvolved in child care—pacing the waiting room floor during childbirth, never changing a diaper or warming a bottle, and generally steering clear of the nursery, leaving the responsibility for childrearing almost entirely up to their wives. Specialized to their role as family breadwinner, these mythical fathers provided a strong but distant model for their children and moral and material support for their wives. Otherwise, these fathers truly were something of a social accident, and hardly active participants in the rearing of their children.

Whether this stereotype of the uninvolved father ever actually existed in large numbers is debatable. Today, there is no single type of father. Some fathers remain uninvolved, others are active participants, and some fathers are even raising children by themselves. A variety of technological, economic, and ideological changes in our society are redefining what it is to be a father. Whether for reasons of personal fulfillment or economic necessity, more women today work full time outside the home than ever before. Women are also returning to work sooner after the birth of a child. As a consequence, fathers are taking on more responsibility for early infant and child care. At one time, kin and clan—that supportive network of aunts and grandparents—could be relied on to help in the care of children as well. Today,

1

the nuclear family is much more isolated because of the high geographic mobility that our economy requires. Legal decisions have affected fathers as well; more divorced fathers than in the past are assuming custody of their children. All of these changes have made it more common for fathers to take an active part in rearing their children.

It is, of course, no accident that just as fathers have moved into a breach created by social circumstances, a new ideology of fatherhood has begun to make inroads into the old stereotype. No longer is the father with a diaper pin in his mouth a comical figure. The ideal father of the newest fashion goes to childbirth class with his wife, coaches her through labor, attends her during delivery, and shares in the care and feeding of the infant, especially when his wife returns to work. No longer a social accident, many fathers are active partners in parenthood and a direct influence on their children's development.

Just how involved the modern father has really become and what are the consequences of this involvement for his children, for his wife, for the life of the family, and for himself are issues that will be addressed in this book. In the last ten years, psychologists and other researchers, undoubtedly stimulated by the new popularity of fathering, have examined a long list of questions about how fathers actually behave with their children and what effects this behavior seems to have on the children's development. It is now clear that fathers can play an important and unique role in the development of the child.

We will look first at the father's role before the birth of the child. Do fathers change during the mother's pregnancy? Do they make psychological adjustments in anticipation of the addition to the family? How does pregnancy change the relationship between husband and wife? Do childbirth classes make a difference in the way fathers experience the birth, and are there any lasting effects on the way they relate to the child? Do fathers who are present during labor and delivery react differently to their newborns? Even if they miss the delivery, fathers are no longer restricted to the traditional peek through the nursery window. How do fathers respond to newborns when they are given the chance to hold and touch them in the hospital? Are fathers similar to mothers in their behavior toward very young babies?

As the child grows older, another set of questions becomes relevant. It is natural to wonder whether boys and girls are affected differently by a father's active involvement. Do fathers treat their daughters and sons differently? If so, in what ways and at what ages? How important is a father's influence on a child's developing sense of sexual identity and social assurance? How can a father influence his child's intellectual development? Most fathers are also husbands. How does their behavior toward their wives affect their children? Some of a father's influence on his children may be indirectly channeled through the mother; the father may affect the mother's feelings and behavior toward the children.

In modern society families exist in a variety of forms. The traditional family arrangement with mother as primary homemaker and caregiver and father as breadwinner is only one of many possible forms of family organization. In many families both parents work, and in a few families mother and father reverse roles so that the mother works outside the home and the father stays home with the children. What are the effects of these arrangements? Our era's high divorce rate creates many single-parent families, and remarriage brings complicated relationships between stepparents and stepchildren. How does divorce affect the father-child relationship? How do single fathers and stepfathers manage the task of child care? Do children develop in different ways when father is the only parent or when they live with their mothers than when both parents are present?

Finally, we will explore how society influences fathers and fathering. What forms of support are available for fathers to help them learn their roles and perform effectively? Fathers are relatively recent objects of study for social scientists, and many of these questions cannot yet be fully answered. Enough is known, however, that we can cast aside many of the myths about fathers.

THEORIES OF FATHERHOOD

Psychology has a long history of ignoring fathers. One of the main reasons for our neglect of fathers lay in our psychological theories of parenthood. Theories are hunches or "best bets" about the way the world probably works. Theorists help us to select the problems and issues that are most likely to further our understanding of children's development. But theorists also constrain us and lead us away from examining some problems in favor of some others. We didn't just forget fathers by accident; we ignored them on purpose because of our assumption that they were less important than mothers in influencing the developing child. Our theories corresponded to the traditional conception of the remote father. Two theorists played particularly important roles in this historical development: Sigmund Freud, the psychoanalyst, and John Bowlby, the British ethologist.

One of Freud's most important and long-lasting contributions was his theory of early social development. According to Freud, different gratifications associated with various body zones (mouth, genitals, and so on) become important at different stages of development. For example, Freud thought that the oral zone and activities associated with eating, suckings, biting, and swallowing are most important to the infant. Since it was the mother who usually fed and cared for the infant — at least in Vienna at the turn of the century — Freud gave the mother a prominent role in infant development. Freud believed that the infant's relationship with his mother significantly shaped his later personality and social relationships. Fathers were virtually ignored. Freud did not consider them an influence in infancy. Fathers did have a place in Freud's theory of development, but not until a later period in childhood. However, many subsequent followers of Freud accepted his emphasis on the importance of infancy for later development and thereby perpetuated his belief that the mother was the primary socializing agent.

The original details of Freud's theory were not accepted by later theorists, but many of his central ideas survived in different form. In the 1940s and 1950s learning theorists like Robert

Sears and John Whiting attempted to translate Freud's ideas into the language of modern theories of learning.[1] These scientists assumed that infants gain satisfaction through the reduction of basic biological drives, such as hunger and thirst. The mother became important to the infant because she was the parent who usually fed it (that is, satisfied its hunger drive). Since fathers were typically less involved in feeding, their role in infant development was assumed to be minimal.

John Bowlby's view of early development differed from Freud's, but the end result was the same — mothers were portrayed as the most important figures in infancy. In the 1940s, Bowlby was a prominent critic of institutions and orphanages where infants and children failed to develop adequate social and emotional behaviors. Along with other influential investigators, among them René Spitz and Margaret Ribble, Bowlby saw "maternal deprivation" as the cause of these developmental problems.[2] He built on these early speculations in his classic paper, "The Nature of the Child's Tie to His Mother," an eloquent plea for the special importance of the mother in her child's early development. In later papers and books, Bowlby continued to develop his argument concerning the importance of the attachment bond — the process by which the infant comes to prefer specific adults, especially his mother, over others.[3] Bowlby suggested that attachment is a result of instinctual responses that are important for the protection and survival of the species. Crying, smiling, sucking, clinging, and following all elicit necessary maternal care and protection for the infant and promote contact between mother and infant. Bowlby stressed that the *mother* is the first and most important object of infant attachment. The mother is biologically prepared to respond to these infant behaviors, just as the infant is predisposed to respond to the sights, sounds, and nurturance provided by his human caretakers. Bowlby believed that it is because of these biologically programmed systems that mother and infant develop attachment to each other. For us, the important message is Bowlby's emphasis on the mother as a central figure in early development. Fathers were simply secondary and at most played a supporting role for the mother.

It is true that throughout Western history fathers have generally taken a minor part in the care and feeding of infants and young children.[4] Anthropological evidence shows, furthermore, that this pattern is by no means unique to the West. In the majority of the world's cultures, mothers are the primary caretakers and the fathers play a lesser role in childrearing.[5] It would be a mistake, however, to conclude that there is anything biologically necessary about maternal caretaking. In a significant minority of the world's cultures, males and females divide the care of young children more evenly. Among the Trobrianders of Melanesia, for example, the father participates actively in the care, feeding, and transport of young children. Similarly, in a number of other cultures including the Taira of Okinawa and the Ilocos of the Philippines, father and mother share more equally in infant and child care. These exceptions suggest that the roles played by mothers and fathers are not biologically predetermined. Instead, the definition of sex roles can vary considerably depending on the social, ideological, and physical conditions in different cultures.

According to another argument, fathers, in contrast to mothers, are biologically ill-equipped to be active contributors to childrearing. The biological uniqueness of maternal caretaking is indicated by the fact that our animal ancestors maintain clear sex-role distinctions, with male monkeys, apes, and baboons generally being uninvolved in infant and child care. For example, Irven DeVore observed cynocephalus baboons in the wild and found that the adult males took little interest in infants.[6] Instead, they played a protective role for the troop as a whole. Studies of rhesus monkeys in captivity tell a similar story. Harry Harlow and his colleagues studied the reactions of male and female monkeys to young infants in a laboratory setting. The males and females played clearly different roles: Females were four times as likely as males to express nurturant behavior to infants, males were ten times as hostile to infants as females.[7] In short, in animals as well as man, there is evidence indicating that males are less involved than females in the care and nurturance of infants.

Not all studies of animal behavior, however, support traditional views of fatherhood. Recent animal evidence has demonstrated that males can assume a fatherly role even with infants. The males of some nonhuman primate species occasionally engage in nurturant caretaking of infants in the wild. Marmosets and tamarins — monkeys who live in Central and South America — are among the most involved monkey fathers. They not only carry infants during the day for the first few months of life, but may chew food for very young infants, and sometimes they even assist during birth. Males of other species of monkeys, such as the Barbary macaques of Asia and Africa, participate in caregiving; they hold, groom, carry, and protect infants. Even male rhesus monkeys, who rarely display parental behavior in the wild, "are certainly capable of doing so when given the opportunity in the laboratory."[8] William Redican housed adult male and infant rhesus monkeys together in the laboratory and found that these males played with and protected the infants and groomed them just as much as mothers generally do. There are, however, wide differences from one species of animal to another, and the extent of male participation in caretaking varies, in part, with the amount of involvement the females will allow. If the mother monkey permits it, males may be more involved. The important point is that the animal evidence does not support the view that paternal behavior is biologically impossible. Even in animal species in which the male typically does not demonstrate active fathering, nurturant paternal behavior can be elicited under the right conditions.

Still another version of the biological argument holds that females are primed to engage in "mothering" by hormonal changes that occur in pregnancy and childbirth. Since fathers do not experience these hormonal changes, the argument suggests, they are not biologically prepared for parenting. Recent animal evidence from Jay Rosenblatt and his colleagues has challenged the necessity of hormones for caretaking.[9] Their careful studies show that both virgin female and male rats will show parenting behavior with sufficient exposure to newborn infants. Thus it seems that environmental conditions can override the effects of hormones, and in the long run, be more important than short-lived hormonal shifts in determining the reactions of males (and females) to infants.

The argument that men are biologically unprepared for parenting clearly cannot be used to justify the limited role that fathers have traditionally played in taking care of infants and children. In short, there is no acceptable theory of fatherhood that necessarily consigns fathers to a secondary role in child care. Nor is there any reason why a parent of either sex should have the greater share of influence on the child's development, although there is every reason to suspect that mothers and fathers will have different kinds of influence on their children. The modern study of fathering has largely turned away from outworn theories of parenthood and toward direct observation of parents and children. We now know a substantial amount about how fathers behave with their children, how this behavior differs from maternal behavior, and just what sorts of influence this behavior can have.

AN ORIENTATION TO UNDERSTANDING FATHERS

Most of us think of fathers as influencing their children directly through their daily face-to-face contact. In turn this suggests to some that fathers must have less influence than mothers because they spend less time with the children. But this does not necessarily follow.

Estimates of the amount of time fathers spend with their infants vary considerably, but most reports indicate that the amount of time is surprisingly limited. In a recent study of middle-class Boston parents, Milton Kotelchuck found that mothers had principal childrearing responsibilities for their 6- to 21-month-old infants. Mothers were present with their infants more than fathers (9 hours versus 3.2 hours per day).[10] Similar patterns are evident in Great Britain.[11] International surveys of how much time fathers and mothers spend on child care confirm these findings. In France and Belgium, for example, mothers spend even more time in child care compared to fathers.[12] But the total time spent with their children is not the most important determinant of the impact of a father or a mother. The sheer *quantity* of time is less important than the *quality* of interaction. Studies of working mothers have consistently shown that the lessened contact as a result of the mother's work time has little effect on children's development.[13] A better predictor of development is how effectively the mother uses her time with her children. Just being available is not the most important dimension. Presumably the same is true for fathers: The real question is not how many hours per day a fathers spends with his child, but what he does with the child when he *is* present.

There is no doubt that fathers can play an important direct role in their children's development. They touch, talk, and tickle, and these are ways of influencing the baby and child. Fathers also manage and organize their children's activities. For example, they may regulate their child's behavior by how they arrange the home environment. Do fathers encourage exploration? Do they permit the infant to crawl around the house and investigate his world? Do they provide interesting toys for the child? Do they make books available as the child begins to read? Do fathers highlight interesting features of the environment by showing and pointing and talking? All of these are ways that a parent manages his child's world and probably changes the child's later social and cognitive development.

Children are not simply passive targets for their father's influence. The father-child relationship is a two-way process, and children influence their fathers just as fathers alter their children's development. Children directly affect the ways that their fathers treat them and thereby contribute to the ways in which they are socialized. The cries of a colicky infant who keeps a father up at night, the plea for understanding from a 4-year-old who has broken a favorite vase, the negotiations of a teenager for the keys to the family car are examples of how children affect fathers' behavior.

Recently we have begun to recognize that the father is important not only through direct influences on his child but also by means of indirect effects on the infant's early interactions with other people. Within the family context, fathers often indirectly

influence their infants and children by affecting the mother's behavior. For example, Frank Pedersen and his colleagues have recently shown that the quality of the husband-wife relationship is
linked to that of the mother-infant relationship.[14] Pedersen observed mothers feeding their 4-week-old infants and assessed
each mother's competence at feeding her baby. Mothers who
were rated highly competent "were able to pace the feeding well,
intersperse feeding and burping without disrupting the baby and
seemed sensitive to the baby's needs for either stimulation of
feeding or brief rest periods during the course of feeding."
Through an interview, Pedersen assessed the husband-wife relationship. His findings are worth quoting: "When the father was
more supportive of the mother, she was more effective in feeding
the baby . . . The reverse holds for marital discord. High tension
and conflict in the marriage was associated with more inept feeding on the part of the mother."[15]

Fathers, as well as mothers, are affected by the quality of the
husband-wife relationship. Couples who argue and criticize each
other are more likely to act this way with their infants. Unfortunately, the reverse does not seem to be true: in Pedersen's study
positive feelings between spouses were unrelated to how affectionate parents were with their babies.

These reflections remind us of an important fact: if we are to
understand the relationship between parent and child, we have
to treat the parents as part of a family system and consider all of
the relationships among the family members. In addition, we
must remember that families do not exist in isolation from other
parts of society. Families are embedded in a wide network of
other social systems, including neighborhoods, communities,
and cultures. In order to understand how fathers function we
need to recognize the influence of the links between families and
these other social systems.[16] By recognizing that fathers are affected by social influences outside the family, we will gain a
clearer understanding of the reasons for the variety of forms that
fatherhood can assume.

Men are affected by fatherhood as well. Being a father can
change the ways that men think about themselves. Fathering

often helps men to clarify their values and to set priorities. It may enhance their self-esteem if they manage its demands and responsibilities well, or alternatively it may be unsettling and depressing by revealing their limitations and weaknesses. Fathers can learn from their children and be matured by them. Maureen Green notes, "One of the first things a father learns from his children is that his needs can match theirs. They look to him for instruction; he can enjoy giving instruction. The children look to him as a model and being a model adds an extra dimension to his decisions. His ambitions and achievements look different to him if he can learn to look at them through their eyes as well as his own."[17] Fathering, in short, may be good for men as well as for children.

2 / The Expectant Father

Becoming a father is not a single event but a gradual process of becoming acquainted with the demands and joys of a new family role. The process begins early. Even before pregnancy, decisions about when and whether to have a child, to go ahead and "try" to become pregnant or to adopt a child are all parts of the complex transition to fatherhood. The process continues as both parents adjust to the mother's pregnancy. Pregnancy is a family affair. Couples, not just mothers, become pregnant. Recently we have begun to recognize that fathers can play important roles during pregnancy.

PREGNANCY AS A FAMILY AFFAIR

The changes that occur for fathers as a result of the mother's pregnancy are not independent of the changes that mothers themselves undergo during pregnancy. In fact, fathers' behavior can best be understood by viewing it in relation to mothers' behavior during pregnancy.

Pregnancy can be conveniently divided into three trimesters or stages, each about three months long. Each phase has its own characteristic problems and pleasures for the expectant couple. For the woman the early stages are often difficult, both psychologically and physically. Nausea, vomiting, fatigue, and headaches are common, and depression, irritability, and anxiety are not unusual. In one study of pregnant couples by Pauline Shereshefsky and Leon Yarrow, "A large proportion of women spoke of tempers more easily aroused, a tendency to be 'edgy,' tense, nervous or 'touchy,' to snap more easily, to become more demanding of their husbands, to dissolve into tears more often — general indications of a greater vulnerability and heightened emotionality."[1] Of course being pregnant is not constantly negative during this period. Many women experience euphoria during these months; some flip back and forth between joy and depression.

In the second trimester of pregnancy, many of the more uncomfortable symptoms disappear. Quickening, the baby's first perceptible movement, usually takes place by the end of the fourth month and is one of the first clear signals that the baby is "on the way." Feeling the baby move can be exciting for both parents. As the baby gets bigger and stronger, though, its movements seem to be more pleasing to fathers than to mothers. In one study of pregnant couples, most of the men said they enjoyed feeling the baby move, but half of the women were not enthusiastic. Obviously, the appeal of fetal movements may depend on whose abdomen is being kicked.[2]

The last trimester of pregnancy is, again, often stressful. By this time the mother has gained approximately 25-30 pounds, and carrying the fetus is tiring and often uncomfortable. The mother often experiences bothersome physical symptoms such as fatigue, insomnia, swollen limbs, and shortness of breath. Perhaps as a result, many pregnant women are anxious and irritable during this period, just as in the first trimester. Additionally, worries about the baby's health and about the process of birth itself may become stronger as birth nears.

How do expectant fathers react during pregnancy? The ways men experience pregnancy and birth vary considerably across cultures. Some primitive cultures mark the transition to fatherhood with special ceremonies. One intriguing phenomenon is called the "couvade" — a term derived from the French word *couver* (which means "to brood" or "to hatch") and coined by the British anthropologist Sir Edward Tylor in 1865:

In certain primitive societies at the approximate time of their wives' lying-in, men take to bed in a pretense ritual, simulating the agony of labor and birth. This ritual serves at least two vital purposes: it establishes for the community just who the father is and also it decoys all evil spirits to the father's hut where they can spend their wrath on the mock mother, leaving the actual mother unharmed to go through the birthing of her baby at a safe distance.[3]

In some cultures, couvade takes on high drama. Consider this example from the Erickala-Vandu, a tribe in Southern India:

Directly the woman feels the birth pangs, she informs her husband who immediately takes some of her clothes, puts them on, places on his forehead the mark the women usually place on theirs, retires into a dark room where there is only a dim lamp, and lies down on the bed, covering himself with a long cloth. When the child is born, it is washed and placed on a cot beside the father.[4]

A Western version of the couvade is what a British psychiatrist, W. H. Trethowan, calls the couvade syndrome: a set of physical symptoms that are experienced by an expectant father and that disappear almost immediately after his wife has given birth. How widespread is the couvade syndrome? Estimates vary considerably, but generally range between 10 and 15 percent of fathers. Many more expectant fathers undergo physical and psychological changes, but not of sufficient magnitude to satisfy a strict definition of the couvade syndrome.

In one examination of the couvade syndrome, Trethowan found that the expectant fathers suffered symptoms such as loss of appetite, toothaches, nausea, and vomiting. The symptoms were most frequent in the third month of pregnancy and then lessened until the final month when there again was an increase. Trethowan also found that these physical symptoms were often accompanied by psychological problems such as depression, tension, insomnia, irritability, and even stuttering. This pattern is very similar to the course of symptoms for mothers, who suffer more morning sickness, headaches, and fatigue in the first and last trimesters of pregnancy than in the middle period. In another study, Beatrice Leibenberg reported that 65 percent of the first-time fathers studied experienced "pregnancy symptoms," including fatigue, nausea, backache, headache, vomiting, and even peptic ulcers.[5]

Although some psychoanalytic writers believe that pregnancy should be viewed as a crisis for most expectant fathers, it is not necessarily a debilitating experience. Nor are all of the changes in men associated with pregnancy quite so dramatic and unsettling. Some, in fact, are more amusing. For example, according to Sam Bittman and Sue Zalk, many men change their appearance during pregnancy — they grow beards or mustaches, or they gain weight.[6] Whether these changes occur because of compassion, empathy, or competition with their wives is not clear.

Physical symptoms are only a small part of the changes that expectant fathers undergo. In anticipation of approaching fatherhood, men during pregnancy show increased interest in babies. Some try to learn about children and parenting by reading books. Many men react to the anticipated financial burden of parenthood by a great increase in work, taking on second jobs, especially during the last few months of pregnancy. Although this increase in work and time away from home is often simply a way of paying for the cribs, cradles, and other baby paraphernalia, some writers, particularly those of a psychoanalytic persuasion, interpret this flurry of activity as a sign of worry and anxiety.

Husbands do worry a lot during pregnancy. In one recent study it was found that men were more anxious than their wives during this period. They even worried more about their wives' aches and pains than their wives did! Fathers also are anxious about some expected things, such as getting to the hospital on time when labor begins and whether the baby will be healthy.[7] Their chief worry is money — to pay the hospital bills, to raise the baby — not an unreasonable concern in view of the fact that the average cost of having a baby is now $1500 in the United States. Estimates of the cost of raising a child to age 18 in the United States range from $85,000 to over $200,000.

Sexual patterns change during pregnancy, too. According to Bittman and Zalk, some men report an increase in sexual attraction to their pregnant wives; others show less interest. Meanwhile the woman's sexual desires may change over the course of the pregnancy. In the first three months, when nausea and irritability are often high, she may not be interested in sex. During the middle trimester, however, her sexual appetite is usually restored. Sexual interest sometimes decreases again in the last stage because of discomfort and fatigue. Although sexual activity is generally not harmful during the later stages of pregnancy, many obstetricians still discourage it. According to William Masters and Virginia Johnson, 77 percent of the women they interviewed were told by their doctors not to have sex during the last trimester.[8] Overall, there is a decrease in sexual relations during pregnancy.

PROVIDING EMOTIONAL SUPPORT

Fathers do not simply show their concern for their wives during pregnancy by having backaches. Men tend to react positively to their pregnant wives' increased need for emotional support. Harold Rausch and his colleagues found that husbands were highly conciliatory during pregnancy.[9] They asked couples to settle a conflict such as what television program to watch. The strategies that the couples used to settle their dispute were observed and analyzed. During pregnancy the husbands were more supportive than husbands in nonpregnant couples, and more supportive than they themselves had been before the pregnancy. Pregnancy is no panacea, however, for unhappy marriages: the emotional support that the husband provided slipped back to its prepregnancy level by the fourth month after the birth. The extra support that the husband does provide during pregnancy is important. In a recent investigation of 26 couples in California, Johanna Gladieux found that emotional support from the husband during pregnancy made it easier for the wife to adjust to pregnancy and enjoy it.[10] Husbands as support figures are particularly important in the early stage of pregnancy — before the public announcement that comes with "showing".

During the second trimester, when pregnancy becomes a public event, friends and relatives become even more important determinants of the expectant mother's satisfaction than the marital relationship. "During this time the acceptance, interest and support of her social community, the opportunity to exchange and share stories or folklore about childbearing and the chance to compare her experiences with others, all become invaluable for the pregnant woman."[11] Parents as well as friends become more important now than in the first trimester: Bittman and Zalk found that 40 percent of the women in their study had more overall contact with their own parents during this period.

Just as the mother looks beyond her spouse for support, information, and reassurance, fathers tend to look for support from friends who are already parents. In addition, expectant fathers turn to their own parents during pregnancy — especially their mothers. "A man may feel he needs more mothering for himself during this stressful period — a little extra stroking at a time when he may feel pressured to be constantly strong and responsible and 'adult' . . . expectant fathers telephoned and wrote letters to their families more during the pregnancy than before."[12] Gladieux found that the availability of these kinds of people, who can serve as experienced guides concerning labor, delivery, and subsequent parenthood, was linked with higher satisfaction for expectant fathers.

Additional evidence concerning the father's importance as a support figure during pregnancy comes from studies that show clear links between the mother's emotional state and early infant development. In one recent study in Boston, infants were found to be less irritable in the first three days after birth if the mother had been calm and relaxed during pregnancy. Moreover, the more positively parents rated their marriage (and presumably how supportive the husband was during pregnancy), the better the infant appeared physiologically at two months, as assessed by such measures as irritability and ability to recover from being upset.[13]

High interest in pregnancy has consequences for later fathering as well. A father's interest in his wife's pregnancy has been found to be positively related to how much he holds the baby in the first six weeks of life and also to whether he attends to the baby when it cries. The husband's attitude also affects his wife's enjoyment of motherhood — the happier he is about the pregnancy, the more she enjoys the first few weeks of the baby's life.[14]

HELPING THE OLDER CHILD

In families with older children, the wife is not the only one who needs support during pregnancy. The father may play a special role in helping the older child adjust to the birth of a new family member. Bittman and Zalk found that over 34 percent of the expectant fathers spent more time with their children during pregnancy than they had before, while only 2 percent reported a decrease. Cecily Legg, Ivan Sherick, and William Wadland found a number of negative reactions in older siblings following the birth of a new baby — including lapses in toilet training, sleep disturbances, and a renewed interest in pacifiers, bottles, and thumbs. They also found that increased involvement of the father during the pregnancy and after the birth helped the older sibling adjust more easily.[15] By "taking up the slack," devoting time and attention to the older child while mother is preoccupied with the new baby, the father helps the older sibling to accept the changed situation.

It is just as well that fathers contribute in this way. Pregnancy makes mothers not only less available but also less patient, and the older children are often the target of their mother's increased irritability. Alfred Baldwin documented these shifts years ago.[16] He found that mothers changed their childrearing style after they became pregnant, spending less time with the older child, behaving less warmly and affectionately, and generally becoming less effective in their childrearing practices. At the same time, they became more restrictive, more severe in their penalties, more coercive, and less democratic. It is not surprising that older children sometimes resent their younger brother or sister!

FATHER'S PRESENCE DURING LABOR AND DELIVERY

Father's involvement in pregnancy doesn't stop at the hospital door. Until only a few years ago, fathers were routinely excluded from participating in childbirth. This exclusion was partly an effort to reduce infection in the delivery unit; fathers were viewed as a possible source of contamination. The waiting room became the celebrated place where father could fret, pace, and sleep, but he could not be with his wife during labor and delivery. Although scenes of pacing fathers in hospital corridors are still commonplace, hospital practices have changed and fathers are no longer strangers in the labor and delivery room. Even as late as 1972, fathers were permitted in the delivery room in only 27 percent of the American hospitals in one survey. Not until 1974 did the American College of Obstetricians and Gynecologists endorse the father's presence during labor. And yet by 1980, fathers were admitted to delivery rooms in approximately 80 percent of American hospitals. Why have things changed?

For one thing, early fears that the father's presence would cause infection proved incorrect.[17] In one survey of 45,000 husband-attended births, there was not a single instance of infection due to the presence of the father in the delivery room. Secondly, parents are demanding more control over the birth process and putting pressure on their obstetricians to change the rules and allow fathers to be present. The way that many parents think about birth has changed. Rather than being treated as a crisis, giving birth is now more often viewed as a normal phase in family development. As part of this shift, many people are seeking to make the process of birth more relaxed. Many hospitals have created birthing rooms, which look very much like comfortable bedrooms and give the impression that the home atmosphere has moved into the hospital.

Here is a description of a birth in one of the New Alternative Birth Centers in San Francisco, which are attempting to introduce a homelike atmosphere in the traditional hospital:

Sarah Katherine Bell was born at 8:56 P.M. Tuesday, May 11, at Mount Zion Hospital. Unlike the experience of her 4-year-old brother, Sarah's first glimpse of the world was not a sterile delivery room bathed in harsh lights and filled with the latest medical equipment, but a room that could have been anyone's bedroom. Her mother, Judy, delivered in a standard double bed with a wicker headboard. Around the bed were plants suspended from macrame hangers, an orange carpet and a sofabed where father could relax when he wasn't coaching his wife's breathing. The lights were low and there was a stereo system for music.

Soon after Sarah's birth, the father picked up the couple's son from a babysitter and brought him to the hospital to meet and touch his new sister. By the next morning the Bells were ready to take their baby home.[18]

This shift to birthing rooms helps to make birth a more normal part of family life while maintaining proper safeguards for the newborn baby and the mother. Fathers feel more welcome in such settings than in the cold, antiseptic, and sterile atmosphere of the traditional delivery room. Because of childbirth education classes, fathers are better prepared not only for what to expect but also for what to do to help the mother during labor and delivery. This may account for the fact that the fears that fathers would "faint" or otherwise be a nuisance were also shown to be ill-founded. Few fathers cause the havoc that obstetricians suspected would occur if the delivery room doors were opened to them.

Childbirth preparation classes are becoming a standard part of the services of most hospitals, and fathers as well as mothers can increasingly be observed doing preparatory exercises and timing breathing patterns. One popular type of preparation for childbirth is the Lamaze method. Future parents attend prenatal classes to learn about the physiological processes of pregnancy and birth. Under the guidance of an instructor, the expectant parents learn and practice breathing exercises appropriate for the different stages of labor. These exercises help the mother to relax and therefore reduce the pain that accompanies the contractions. The father plays a supporting role in this process. Robert Fein interviewed fathers after childbirth and found that they reported several ways in which they had helped their wives during labor and delivery:

Men timed contractions, breathed along with their wives to help them stay "on top" of contractions, massaged backs, brought ice chips and juice, translated and transmitted requests from their wives to doctors and nurses, gave constant caring attention and encouragement and were consistent reminders to their wives when the labor was most difficult that the women were not alone and that labor would end.[19]

Another benefit of training for birth is that mothers who have learned these relaxing skills require less medication for pain during labor and delivery. This is especially true if fathers are also present during the delivery. Using medication during birth has effects on the baby, causing drowsiness, lethargy, and even possibly poor attention; therefore, reducing the need for medication is a positive benefit to the child. However, not all investigators have agreed that childbirth classes themselves reduce the need for drugs. A self-selection factor may operate: only certain types of people take the classes, particularly the better-educated. Perhaps such people would do well in childbirth and need less medication whether they attended these classes or not. Recent evidence makes this explanation seem unlikely, however. A group of investigators in Germany assigned some women to a childbirth preparation group and others to a control group who received no preparation. The results were striking: the "prepared" women had shorter labors, needed less medication, and reported enjoying the birth experience more than the women who had not received preparation for childbirth.

It is not clear that the classes *alone* always yield benefits such as making labor and delivery easier. Recent research has shown that childbirth preparation has an effect by making it more likely that fathers will be present during labor and delivery. The father's presence may be a necessary ingredient to the effectiveness of childbirth preparation classes. William Henneborn and Rosemary Cogan studied two groups of couples, all of whom had attended childbirth education classes. In one group the fathers were present throughout labor and delivery; in the other group the fathers attended only the first stage of labor. The women whose husbands participated in both labor and delivery reported less pain, received less medication, and felt more positive about the birth experience than the women in the other group.[20]

Other investigators confirm that the father's presence is significant in the birth process. Doris Entwisle and Susan Doering compared deliveries in which the husband was present during the second stage of labor with deliveries in which he was not. The father's presence increased the mother's emotional experiences at the birth; mothers reported the birth as a "peak" experience more often if the father was present. Not surprisingly, being present and being actively involved in the delivery affected the quality of the father's experience too. Sharing the delivery was more important to men than being in the labor room. Of the husbands in the Entwisle and Doering study who were not in the delivery room, 88 percent felt negative about missing the delivery. One said "I felt anxious. Very anxious. Boy it's taking a long time. And disappointed, like I'd let her down. Because I heard her — a nurse came out, and I heard my wife saying, 'I want my husband!' and I thought: Oh, God what's happening? I felt like — possibly — I hadn't done my job. I don't know why he [the doctor] made me leave." Those who were present were enthusiastic about the experience — 95 percent of them were positive. As one man put it, "I felt tremendous. It was just an experience I'd never — had before and it's a good experience. I felt like I was part of it too. I was feeling great, tremendous."[21]

Overall, the fathers' reaction at the moment of birth was more positive than their wives'. This may not be surprising — fathers had experienced no physical pain and had been given no dulling drugs. In comparison, fathers who spent time in the waiting room were generally neutral in their emotional reaction to the news of the birth. Only the fathers who were present were positive, and about a quarter of them reported an "ecstatic peak experience"; none of the fathers in the waiting room reached this emotional peak. As one elated father put it, "As joyful as I've ever been in my life. That is — the greatest experience of anything I've ever done. It was just — a very happy time — a feeling I've never had before."[22]

Being present at the child's birth has other advantages for fathers: in this same study, more fathers (51 percent) than mothers (25 percent) held their babies while still in the delivery room. As the investigators noted, "The father, of course, is not lying down with an intravenous tube inserted in one arm and perhaps a blood pressure cuff on the other."[23] In view of the real possibility that early contact with babies may strengthen feelings of fatherhood, being present at the delivery may facilitate later involvement with the infant. Of course, the husband's experience is closely tied to his wife's experience. Women who have a positive birth experience contribute to their husbands' enjoyment of the birth. In sum, preparation for childbirth leads to more active participation by fathers in labor and delivery, which, in turn, makes the whole birth event better for both mother and father — and perhaps gets the father's relationship with his infant off to a better start.

More radical innovations aimed at increasing the father's involvement in the birth process are being tried on an experimental basis. A team of New Jersey obstetricinas, Myron Levine and Robert Block, encourage fathers to "play doctor" for the day and deliver their babies themselves (in normal, uncomplicated births) under the supervision of the obstetrician.[24] Their intent is "to bring the home aspect into the safety of the hospital setting and to make giving birth more family — centered." Fathers who deliver their babies are enthusiastic: some typical comments are "On a real high!" "Pretty fantastic!" "As if I'd just caught the winning pass in the superbowl!" These dads also become more involved in the daily care of their infants at home. Three months after the delivery, more than twice as many of the fathers who had delivered their infants were spending an hour or more with their babies daily, compared to fathers who had not delivered their babies. Although these results are intriguing, we cannot leap to conclusions. Most of the fathers were volunteers, and it is possible that only the fathers who were *already* likely to be highly involved with their babies agreed to help out in the delivery.

FATHERS AND CESAREAN CHILDBIRTH

The father's presence has positive effects during Cesarean deliveries as well. Fathers are increasingly being allowed to be present during Cesarean deliveries. When regional anesthesia is used, the mother can remain conscious and alert, able to benefit from her husband's presence in the same way that vaginally delivered mothers do. According to a recent study of women whose babies were delivered by Cesarean section, women whose husbands were present during delivery were more positive about the birth experience than women whose husbands were not present.[25] In the near future, fathers are no longer likely to be excluded from the Cesarean deliveries, and in view of the benefits, this is a promising trend.

Surprisingly, perhaps, Cesarean delivery — regardless of whether or not the father is present in the delivery room — affects the relationship between father and infant. Frank Pedersen and his colleagues observed the impact of Cesarean delivery of the father-infant relationship five months after birth.[26] In contrast to the fathers of infants who were delivered vaginally, the "Cesarean" fathers spent more time in routine care and feeding of their infants in the home. Why? Cesarean delivery implies a variety of changes for the family. The father may be pressed into service earlier because mothers who deliver by Cesarean take longer to recover than those who deliver vaginally. The mother is tired and unable to carry as much of the burden of newborn care, and so the father takes over some of these duties. There is other evidence, from a Swedish study by John Lind, that fathers who are permitted to care for the baby (to feed and diaper it) in the hospital do more caretaking in the home three months later.[27] Together these studies suggest that roles that are organized early after birth may persist, at least for a time. Mode of delivery — vaginal versus Cesarean — may have major consequences for the level of involvement between father and infant. Whether greater involvement by the father affects the child's development will be explored in a later chapter.

Looking at pregnancy from the perspective of the couple rather than considering it an experience that happens to the mother alone has made us aware of the myriad ways that fathers participate in pregnancy. Not only do they offer comfort and support to their wives, but they go through a process of defining for themselves what it means to become a father. Shifts in hospital practices are allowing fathers to participate more actively in childbirth, and couples vary widely in how much they take advantage of this new option. To date the evidence suggests that fathers who choose to become more involved in pregnancy and childbirth seem to benefit themselves, their wives, and even their infants.

3 / Fathers and Infants

The days when fathers were permitted no more than a glance at their new offspring through the nursery window are past in most hospitals. Many more fathers are now permitted to have direct contact with their babies in the hospital rather than waiting until they go home. Now that fathers and newborns are getting together more frequently, researchers are watching more often. The aim is to determine whether fathers and mothers differ in their early interaction with their young infants. Traditionally, it was assumed that fathers were uninterested and uninvolved with newborn babies, but recent studies suggest a very different picture. Martin Greenberg and Norman Morris were among the first researchers to notice how delighted and pleased fathers are with their newborns. They interviewed new fathers and discovered that "fathers begin developing a bond to their newborn by the first three days after birth and often earlier. Furthermore, there are certain characteristics of this bond which we call 'engrossment' . . . a feeling of preoccupation, absorption and interest in their newborn."[1]

Although these interviews are suggestive, such verbal evidence needs to be supplemented by direct observations of fathers with their babies to determine whether these self-reports of feelings and interest are reflected in actual behavior. A series of my own studies helps put the issue on a firmer basis.[2] Instead of asking fathers how they feel about their newborns, Sandra O'Leary and I observed the fathers when they joined mother and baby in the mother's hospital room. The results were clear: as shown by a wide variety of parenting behaviors such as touching, holding, kissing, exploring, and imitating the infant, fathers were just as interested in their babies as were mothers. In fact, fathers tended to hold the infant more than mothers and to rock the infant in their arms more than mothers.

This study by itself, however, does not provide conclusive evidence that fathers are involved with their infants. For one thing, since both mother and father were in the room, the high degree of father-infant interaction might have been due to the supporting presence of the mother, who might have encouraged the father and provided physical assistance and verbal instructions. Second, most of the fathers in this study had attended childbirth classes and had been present during the delivery. They therefore might have been more interested in their parental role and more likely to involve themselves with their infants than other fathers. Third, the men we observed were middle class and well educated; perhaps fathers in lower-income families tend to define parental roles more rigidly and therefore to treat their new babies differently.

To investigate these questions, we studied lower-class fathers who had not participated in childbirth classes and had not been present during delivery. We observed the father alone with the infant, the mother alone with the infant, and the father, mother, and infant together. Again, the fathers were interested and active participants in the first few days after delivery. Whether alone with their newborn or together with their wife and baby, the fathers were just as nurturant and stimulating as the mothers. The only nurturant behavior in which mothers surpassed fathers was smiling. However, it has been well established that women smile more than men, not just at babies but at all kinds of people.

Being nurturant, affectionate, and loving may be good for fathers as well as for babies. The opportunities to express these emotions to their children may allow men to become more expressive and gentle in their relationships with other people too. Whether men really do change in this way after becoming a father, however, is not yet known.

The father can also indirectly affect his infant by influencing the way in which the mother treats her infant. We observed an example of this kind of indirect influence in a comparison of mothers alone with their babies and mothers with their babies when their husbands were also present. In the fathers' presence mothers stimulated the babies less — talking, touching, and holding them less often. However, they also smiled at the babies and "explored" them (by counting toes, checking ears, feeling the baby's head, and so on) more often when their husband was with them. This suggests that the father's presence may increase the mother's interest in their new baby.

Recently, David Phillips and I took a closer look at the types of speech that fathers and mothers use in talking to their newborns.[3] Talking to babies is different from talking to adults, and earlier researchers have found that mothers use a special form of speech when talking to babies. Often called "motherese," it is characterized by slow and exaggerated speech, lots of repetition, and short phrases.[4] Catchwords such as *hey, hi,* and *hello* are often part of motherese. To discover whether fathers make these same kinds of speech adjustments when they talk to babies, we recorded fathers' speech while they were either feeding or playing with their newborns. We found that just as mothers adjust their speech, so do fathers. In contrast to the way they talk to other adults, fathers slow their rate of speech, shorten their phrases, and repeat words and phrases much more when they talk to their newborn infants. This "baby talk" probably helps to attract and maintain the baby's attention better than talking in a normal adult voice. If this is true, it may help babies learn to recognize their parents' and other caregivers' faces and voices. Whatever the answer, the study does provide another piece of evidence that fathers are sensitive to infants. Like mothers, they talk to babies at the baby's level.

Some men pay much more attention to babies than others do. What distinguishes men who coo and fuss over new babies — other people's babies as well as their own — from men who show little interest? One clue comes from Sandra Bem, who suggests that our definitions of how masculine or feminine we are may affect how nurturant we are willing to be.[5] She argues the normal adults are not either masculine *or* feminine, but have some combination of traits traditionally considered masculine and feminine. Therefore some men are tough and assertive (traditional masculine traits) as well as sensitive and empathic (traditional feminine traits). Bem calls individuals who rate themselves high on both masculinity and feminity "androgynous." To find out if the way we perceive our sex role affects our treatment of infants, she watched men who differed in their sex-role perceptions interact with 5-month-old babies. She found that androgynous men showed more interest, approached closer to the baby, and smiled, touched, and vocalized at the baby more than men who viewed themselves as traditionally masculine.

The amount of interest men show toward infants and children also varies across the life span, depending on the role a man is playing at a particular time in his life.[6] Adolescent males are not very responsive to babies, but, not surprisingly, men show increased interest in babies when they become parents. Fathers' responsiveness to infants tends to diminish slightly after their own children have grown up and left home. However, when men reach their second "fatherhood" as grandfathers, they again become interested in babies. Men have a clear capacity for nurturance, and becoming a father or a grandfather often increases their nurturant behavior.

READING THE BABY'S MESSAGES

Other evidence indicates that fathers are not just actively involved with their infants but are competent social partners as well. One part of being a competent social partner is recognizing and correctly labeling the baby's signals. Infants cry, move, smile, and fuss, and parents need to be able to interpret the different signals. Are fathers as sensitive as mothers to these signals?

A recent series of studies by Ann Frodi, Michael Lamb, and their colleagues helps to provide an answer. They measured sensitivity to infant behavior by using psychophysiological measures such as heart rate and blood pressure as well as the parents' own reports of how they felt about the infant behavior. Both mothers and fathers perceived an infant cry as unpleasant, while the sight of a smiling, gurgling infant elicited positive feelings. The psychophysiological measures tell a similar story: blood pressure rose in response to the crying infant but not in reaction to the smiling baby. Most important, the physiological reactions of mothers and fathers were not different. These data contradict the claim that women but not men are innately predisposed to respond to infant signals. As the researchers put it, "Our data do not prove that there are no biological sex differences, but they do speak against the notion that 'maternal' responsiveness reflects predominantly biological influences."[7]

Fathers, like mothers, are capable of discriminating among different types of crying patterns. The cry of a premature infant, for instance, differs from the cry of a full-term baby; it is shrill and high pitched. When listening to tapes of premature and full-term babies crying, both mothers and fathers found the cry of the premature infant more unpleasant than the cry of a full-term baby.[8] Even more impressive are data that indicate that men and women are equally able to discriminate among different crying patterns. Babies of course, cry for various reasons: because they are hungry, or because a pin is pricking them; and so on. Peter Wolff has shown that a mother's reaction — whether she feeds, picks up, or ignores her crying baby — will depend on her reading of the meaning of its cry. A number of years ago Olé Wasz-Hockert and his colleagues in Sweden found that mother and other women could tell the difference between different types of cries.[9] Can men do the same? According to my own research, male college students, who are not yet fathers, can tell the cries apart just as well as childless females. Thus men appear to be as sensitive as women in interpreting this type of infant signal.

There is more to a successful interchange than merely recognizing the baby's signals. The competent caretaker must learn to react appropriately to a baby's messages by behaving responsively. As in any other form of social interaction, stimulation alone is not sufficient. The timing or pacing of a person's behavior is just as important as the amount and kind of stimulation he provides.

Fathers not only are able to recognize infant signals, but also are able to use these signals appropriately to guide their own behavior. In my studies of fathers and newborns I have consistently found that fathers are just as responsive as mothers to infant signals such as sounds and mouth movements.[10] Both mothers and fathers talk to the infant more, touch the infant more, and look more closely at the infant after an infant vocalization. Fathers, however, are more likely than mothers to respond to infant vocalization by talking to the baby, while mothers are more likely to react with touching. Perhaps during feeding, fathers are more cautious than mothers about touching the baby, for fear of disrupting the feeding. The baby's mouth movements, like vocalizations, get responses from both parents: both fathers and mothers increase their talking, touching, and stimulation in response to mouth movements. These data indicate that both fathers and mothers react to the newborn infant's cues in a sensitive and functional manner even though they differ in their specific responses. As the infant develops, parents do differ in their reaction to some signals, such as smiling. Just as mothers smile at their newborn infants more than fathers do, when infants begin to smile, mothers react to their smiles more than fathers do.[11]

Together these findings remind us that the relationship between father and infant works in both directions. Fathers and infants, just like mothers and infants, continually influence each other. Fathers react to babies' signals, and babies, in turn, learn to use their developing communication skills to affect the ways their fathers treat them. These exchanges teach infants an early and important lesson in social control: that they can influence other people through their own behavior.

ROLE DIFFERENTIATION BEGINS EARLY

Although I have emphasized the lack of differences between mothers and fathers, there is one difference that should be mentioned. While mothers and fathers are equally involved with their babies from the beginning, fathers are more likely to be found playing with their infants than feeding them. Mothers, according to observational studies—even mothers of bottle-fed babies—spend more time in feeding and related caretaking activities, such as wiping the baby's face, than do fathers. From the earliest days of the baby's life, clear parental role division is evident. This traditional division of roles is found even in families where the couples hold egalitarian views. This finding seems to reflect a more general tendency: pregnancy and the birth of a first child often shift a couple toward a more traditional division of roles. This is confirmed by a recent study by Carolyn Cowan and her colleagues of couples during pregnancy and up to six months after the birth of a first child.[12] They found that couples shifted toward a traditional arrangement in a variety of areas such as household tasks, decisionmaking, and baby care—regardless of whether their prior role division had been traditional or egalitarian.

Most evidence suggests that this pattern persists well beyond the hospital stay and the newborn period. In a recent study in Boston, Milton Kotelchuck found that mothers spent an average of an hour and a half per day feeding their year-old infants, compared to 15 minutes for fathers. Of course, most of the fathers were not present at home during the day, and most of the mothers were. But that is not the only reason for the difference. Seventy-five percent of the fathers had no regular responsibilities for taking care of their infants, and 43 percent reported they had never changed their babies' diapers. Nor is this a uniquely American picture. Martin Richards and his colleagues have reported similar findings for Great Britain. Only 35 percent of the fathers in their study regularly fed their 30-week-old infants. By the time the infants passed their first birthday, 40 percent of the fathers were regularly helping with feeding.[13]

Fathers do participate in infant care more actively under some circumstances. As I noted in Chapter 2, fathers spend more time in caregiving when mothers have had a Cesarean delivery. Another situation that may increase fathers' role in early caregiving is the birth of a baby prematurely. Having a baby earlier than expected can be stressful for the family, thereby increasing the importance of the father's support for the mother. Investigators in both England and the United States have recently found that fathers of premature infants are more active in feeding, diapering, and bathing their infants than fathers of full-term babies, both in the hospital and later at home.[14] These fathers' more active participation in caregiving is particularly helpful because premature infants usually need to be fed more often than full-term infants and experience more feeding disturbances. Premature infants also can be less satisfying to feed and to interact with, because they are often less responsive to parental stimulation than full-term infants.[15] Thus by sharing more than usual in caregiving, the father of a premature infant relieves the mother of some of this responsibility, giving the mother some much-needed rest, and thereby may indirectly influence the baby by positively affecting the relationship between mother and baby. The father's support is important in other ways as well. Often a premature infant is kept in the hospital for a period of time, and the father can play an important role by visiting and becoming acquainted with the baby during this period. Recent research in Canada by Klaus Minde has shown that mothers who have supportive husbands tend to visit their premature babies in the hospital more often, and that mothers who visit more have fewer parenting problems later than mothers who visit less frequently.[16] Again we see that fathers can influence their infants by affecting the mother-infant relationship. Understanding the father's role in infant development clearly requires that the father's behavior be viewed in the context of his role within the family.

Even with full-term infants, individual families vary considerably in how mothers and fathers divide responsibility for child care. In a recent study of Austrailian fathers, Graeme Russell found that a man's sex-role orientation was an important factor in how much he participated in diaper changing, feeding, and other caretaking routines. Using Sandra Bem's measure of sex-role androgyny, described earlier, Russell found that the fathers who were androgynous — who described themselves as having both masculine and feminine traits, such as assertiveness and sensitivity — participated more in daily child care than did fathers who described themselves as masculine. The androgynous men took responsibility for daily care 25 percent of the time, while the mascuine men participated less than 10 percent of the time in dressing, feeding, bathing, and diapering. The androgynous fathers also interacted with their children more overall, playing with them and reading them stories more often than did the more "masculine" fathers.[17]

Wives' expectations about their husband's behavior make a difference, too. Even the men who viewed themselves as masculine — tough, strong, and assertive — changed diapers more often if they were married to an androgynous woman or a woman who viewed herself as masculine. Only when a stereotypically masculine man was married to a woman who viewed herself as stereotypically feminine could he avoid the diaper detail or the feeding routine. Russell's work reminds us that families distribute child-care tasks in various ways. In the families he studied, however, mothers were still the primary caregivers, and even the androgynous men played a clearly secondary role in child care.

Are fathers the secondary caregivers because they are less talented at child care than mothers? When Douglas Sawin and I tested this hypothesis, it turned out to be wrong. We observed mothers and fathers feeding their babies and measured the amount of milk consumed. The babies took almost the same amount from fathers as from mothers.[18] But of course there is more to being a competent caregiver than merely getting food into a baby. As explained earlier, parental competence is best measured by how sensitively parents interpret and respond to infant cues and signals. To illustrate, take the feeding situation. The aim of the caregiver is to ensure that the infant continues to receive enough milk. By behaviors such as sucking, pausing, coughing, or spitting up, infants indicate whether the feeding is going smoothly or whether some adjustment is in order. One way to measure how capable parents are as feeders is to examine how quickly they modify their behavior in response to the infant's distress signals. Sawin and I observed fathers and mothers feeding their babies and found that fathers were just as sensitive to these signals as mothers. Fathers, like mothers, responded to these infant cues by momentarily stopping the feeding, looking more closely to check on the baby, and speaking to the baby. The only difference between mothers and fathers was that fathers were less likely than mothers to stimulate their babies by touching them when the baby signaled that there was a momentary difficulty. Although they tend to spend less time feeding their babies, fathers are as sensitive and responsive as mothers to infant cues in the context of feeding.

If fathers are so competent at feeding infants, why don't they do it more often? One reason may be that parents do not believe fathers have this ability. In another recent Australian study, Graeme Russell found that 51 percent of mothers and 71 percent of fathers believed in a "maternal instinct" with regard to child care.[19] And while 60 percent of the mothers felt that their husbands had the ability to care for children, only 34 percent of the fathers considered themselves capable of taking care of their children. Moreover, most fathers perceived their role as beginning after the baby stage and believed that the father's role is more important later in the child's life, especially during adolescence.

Even when fathers do not participate directly in feeding their babies, they can still influence the success of feeding in indirect ways, through their relationship with the mother. In Chapter 1, I discussed Frank Pedersen's finding that mothers who had tense and conflicted relationships with their husbands were not as skilled in feeding their babies. Father's indirect influences can be observed in other ways as well. Consider the father's role when the mother is breastfeeding. Researchers Doris Entwisle and Susan Doering found that mothers who were supported in their breastfeeding efforts continued to breastfeed longer than mothers with less supportive husbands.[20] Fathers, of course, can be helpful when mothers are breastfeeding by sharing in other caregiving activities such as bathing and diapering, and occasionally relieving mother of her feeding responsibilities by giving the infant supplemental bottles. In sum, fathers can influence their babies, as well as their wives, by both direct and indirect contributions to early feeding.

PLAY

Play is one of the chief occupations of infants and children. Play begins very early in infancy, and babies are well prepared for playful interaction with other humans. Recent research on perception indicates that babies are particularly responsive to faces and voices of humans. As Rudolph Schaffer recently noted:

> From the beginning of life, [the infant] is able to regulate what he takes in by selective attention. Given the choice, he will seek out those features of his surroundings to which, by virtue of his physical make-up he is most sensitive . . . If we were to design an object that would contain all these features and thus be maximally attention-worthy, we would end up with a human being . . . It is as though the infant is biologically "set" to be triggered by certain quite specific yet primitive stimuli — stimuli found in other human beings, and one can, of course, readily understand that it would be biologically useful for a baby to be prepared from the very beginning for interaction with other human beings.[21]

Just as babies respond to the sight of a human face, they are more likely to respond to human voices than to other types of sounds.

Both fathers and mothers are active playmates for the infant. In fact, though mothers contribute to their infant's development in a wide variety of ways, fathers probably make their contribution primarily through play. If the mother is not working outside the home, she probably spends more total time in playing with her baby than the father does. However, fathers devote a higher proportion of their time with the baby to play than mothers. For example, in his study of middle-class Boston families, Milton Kotelchuck found that fathers devote nearly 40 percent of their time with their infants to play, while mothers spend about 25 percent of their time in play.[22] In contrast, mothers who stay home with their children generally caretake as much as they play. Fathers are usually secondary caregivers, but they do have an important role as play partners.

In a recent study of English parents, Martin Richards and his colleagues found that play was the most common activity for fathers of 30- and 60-week-old infants. In fact, 90 percent of the fathers played regularly with their infants, while less than half participated in caretaking. The situation is similar in the United States. Michael Lamb and his associates watched mothers and fathers interacting with their infants at 7-8 months of age and again at 12-13 months. There were marked differences in the reasons that led fathers and mothers to pick up their infants: fathers were more likely to hold their babies to play with them, while mothers were more likely to hold them for caretaking purposes such as feeding and bathing.[23]

However, fathers are not always the primary playmate, according to Frank Pedersen and his colleagues[24] Observing mothers and fathers with their 5-month-old infants, they found that fathers played more than mothers only if the father was employed and the mother did not hold a job outside the home. In families where both parents were employed, mothers played more than fathers. Since the observations took place in the evenings after both parents came home from their jobs, Pedersen suggests that the mother played more as a way of reestablishing contact with her baby after being away from home for the day. One result was that fathers in these two-earner families had less play time with their infants. Family work organization clearly can affect father's status as primary playmate. Whether or not these mothers continue to be as active play partners as the baby grows older, however, remains unanswered.

Do fathers and mothers have different styles of play? Consider these two examples: Father picks up 7-month-old Nathan, tosses him in the air, and throws his head back so that he and Nathan are face to face. As Nathan giggles and chortles, father lowers him, shakes him, and tosses him up in the air again. Mother sits 10-month-old Lisa on her lap and pulls out her favorite toy, a green donkey that brays when you squeeze it. Lisa smiles, and for the next few minutes mother moves the donkey in front of Lisa's eyes, makes it bray, and talks and sings to her daughter. Lisa watches intently, smiles, and occasionally reaches for her donkey. Are these examples merely cultural stereotypes, or do mothers and fathers really play with their babies in different ways?

A series of recent studies confirm that these differences in parental play styles do exist. Michael Yogman, T. Berry Brazelton, and their colleagues explored differences in mother's and father's play by studying five infants from the ages of 2 weeks to 24 weeks.[25] In a laboratory setting, they observed each infant with three different play partners: father, mother, and a stranger. The infant was placed in a reclining chair (or baby seat) and the face-to-face interactions that developed between the infant and the adult as they play together were filmed. There were clear differences in the ways the adults played with the infants, as revealed by talking and touching patterns. Mothers spoke softly, repeating words and phrases frequently and imitating the infant's sounds more than either fathers or strangers. A burst-pause pattern was common for these mothers: a rapidly spoken series of words and sounds, followed by a short period of silence. Fathers were less verbal and more tactile than mothers. They touched their infants with rhythmic tapping patterns more often than mothers or strangers. Father-infant play shifted rapidly from peaks of high infant attention and excitement to valleys of minimal attention, while mother-infant play demonstrated more gradual shifts. As Brazelton commented:

> Most fathers seem to present a more playful, jazzing up approach. As one watches this interaction, it seems that a father is expecting a more heightened, playful response from the baby. And he gets it! Amazingly enough, an infant by two or three weeks displays an entirely different attitude (more wide-eyed, playful and bright faced) toward his father than to his mother. The cycles might be characterized as higher, deeper, and even a bit more jagged.[26]

Even though fathers and mothers differ in style in their early face-to-face play, they both show a high degree of sensitivity to their babies. Both the mother's and the father's play is characterized by reciprocity: the parent and infant engage in a dialogue with a clear cycle of approach and withdrawal on the part of both players. With young infants, the parents probably contribute most to this reciprocity; they elicit the baby's attention, gauge their behavior to keep the baby interested, and reduce their level of stimulation when the baby is tired or bored. As infants get older they develop more skill in adjusting their behavior to keep the interaction going. Jerome Bruner has recently demonstrated that one-year-old infants can play turn-taking games, which rely on each partner doing his part to keep the interchange alive.[27]

Mothers and fathers also have different styles of play with older infants and in situations other than face-to-face play. Thomas Power and I examined the types of games that fathers and mothers played with their 8-month-old infants in a laboratory playroom.[28] Unlike the earlier studies of face-to-face play, this situation was relatively unstructured and toys were available for the parents and infants to use. We were able to identify a number of distinctive games that were played. These range from "distal" games, which involve stimulating the baby at a distance by shaking or showing a toy, to "physical" games, which involve directly touching, lifting, or bouncing the baby. Other games, such as grasping and retrieving games, require the infant to hold or retrieve a nearby toy.

Mothers and fathers play many of the same games, but there are clear differences in their styles. Fathers engaged in significantly more physical games, such as bouncing and lifting, than mothers. Mothers, in contrast, used a more distal, attention-getting approach and played more watching games. A favorite game of the mothers was to show the baby a toy and then shake and move it to stimulate the baby. Fathers were particularly likely to play "lifting" games with their boy infants and were less physical with their girls.

These differences between mothers' and fathers' styles of play are found in the home as well as in the laboratory. Observing infants from 8 to 24 months of age, Michael Lamb found that fathers engaged in more physical games such as rough-and-tumble play and more unusual or idiosyncratic games than mothers. Mothers, in contrast, engaged in more conventional play activities (such as peek-a-boo and pat-a-cake), stimulus-toy play (jiggling a toy to stimulate the child), and reading than fathers. As one researcher, K. Alison Clarke-Stewart, recently put it: "Fathers' play was relatively more likely to be physical and arousing rather than intellectual, didactic or mediated by objects — as in the case of the mothers."[29] Infants get not just more stimulation from their fathers, but a qualitatively different pattern of stimulation.

Fathers do not show this predominantly physical style of play with all types of infants. In a recent study, my colleagues and I observed how fathers and mothers behave with full-term infants in contrast to infants born prematurely. (In the United States approximately 14 percent of all infants are born prematurely.) Both in the hospital and soon after these infants were brought home, fathers exhibited their characteristic higher rate of physical play only with full-term infants. Fathers did not play with preterm infants in this physical manner. Whether or not fathers continue to play differently with preterm infants as they develop is still being evaluated. Perhaps they begin to play more physically when their premature baby is older and perceived as more robust.

Games that fathers and mothers play may have an important impact on the child's later social and cognitive development. Some games have short-term effects; their main purpose is to engage the infant's attention and maintain the social interaction between parent and infant. Watching, toy touching, and bouncing and lifting games are play of this type. Other games may affect the infant's long-term development. Grasping and retrieving games, for example, may help the infant learn to explore objects or the larger environment. Face-to-face games may teach the infant turn-taking skills and provide early lessons in control of the social environment. As we will see in later chapters, fathers, more than mothers, seem to affect their child's later development mainly through their play.

Why do mothers and fathers play differently? Do the differences have a biological basis, or are they due to environmental influences? Experience with infants, the amount of time routinely spent with infants, the usual kind of responsibilities (caretaking versus play) that a parent assumes—all of these factors may significantly affect the parent's style of play regardless of sex. Tiffany Field recently compared fathers who serve as primary caretakers—a trend in family organization that is on the increase in the United States—with fathers who are secondary caretakers, the traditional father's role.[30] Using the same face-to-face interaction situation that I described earlier, she found that the two groups of fathers played with their infants differently. Primary-caretaker fathers smiled more and imitated their babies' facial expressions and high-pitched vocalizations more than secondary-caretaker fathers. In these ways they acted very much like mothers who are primary caretakers. Being a primary caretaker and, therefore, spending more time with the baby seems significantly to affect the fathers' style of play—a reminder that fathers' behavior can be modified and is not entirely biologically determined. However, not all aspects of the fathers' play style changed. The primary-caretaker fathers were just as physical as the secondary-caretaker fathers, which means that there may be limits on how much fathers' typical style can be altered. Mothers' distinctive verbal play style shows the same kind of persistence across different forms of family organization. In Pedersen's study of mothers who worked outside the home, mothers played more but did not change their style of play.[31] The working mothers stimulated their babies verbally more than before; they did not become more like fathers and play more physically with their babies. Whether these distinctively female and male play styles are due to cultural influences or biological factors remains a puzzle for future researchers to solve. However, the fact that male monkeys show the same rough-and-tumble physical style of play as human fathers suggests that we cannot ignore a possible biological component in play styles of mothers and fathers.

These differences in parental play styles are not lost on the infants. Infants appear to respond more positively to play with their fathers than to play with their mothers. In one study,

K. Alison Clarke-Stewart gave 2½-year-olds a choice of play partners, and more than two-thirds of the children chose to play with their fathers rather than their mothers. Other evidence suggests that a child's preference for play with one parent or the other may depend on whether the child is a boy or girl. According to David Lynn, while boys always clearly prefer their fathers as playmate, girls between 2 and 4 years of age show a shift away from father to mother as a preferred play partner.[32] This shift may occur because as girls develop they become increasingly attentive to their mother as a model for learning female sex-role behavior.

Both mothers and fathers are important play partners, but they may have different types of effects on their baby's development. The father's physical stimulation complements the mother's verbal interaction. It is not yet clear how each of these separate components contributes to the infant's development.

THE INFANT'S SEX AND FATHER'S BEHAVIOR

Before their baby is born, many parents have a clear preference for a boy or a girl—especially if the infant is to be their first child. Both mothers and fathers prefer boys, not just in the United States and Britain, but in India, Brazil, and a variety of other countries as well. This preference is particularly strong in men; between three and four times as many men prefer boys as prefer girls. Reproduction patterns are influenced by these preferences. According to Lois Hoffman, who conducted an extensive survey of 1500 women and 400 men, couples are more likely to continue to have children if they have only girls. They will have more children than they had originally planned in order to try for a boy.[33]

If parents and particularly fathers prefer sons, do they treat them any differently from daughters once they are born? Fathers do treat male and female infants differently—even in the newborn period. In a study of behavior in the hospital, fathers touched and vocalized most with their boys. Not only do fathers talk more to their boys, they are also more likely to respond to their son's vocalizations. These patterns are particularly marked for first-born boys. Girls are not ignored by their parents: according to Evelyn Thoman and her colleagues, mothers are more active stimulators of girls. In their studies of mothers and newborns during feeding they found that mothers talked to and touched their daughters more than their sons.[34]

This pattern is not restricted to the first few days after the baby is born. In our observations of fathers at home with their infants at three weeks and three months of age, Sawin and I found that fathers continue to treat boys and girls differently.[35] In a play situation, fathers consistently stimulated their sons more than their daughters. Fathers touched their sons and visually stimulated them by showing them a toy more often than their daughters. Fathers even looked at their boys more often than their girls. Of course fathers did play with their daughters, but it was the mothers who were the main source of stimulation for the baby girls in this study. Mothers more frequently stimulated their daughters with the toy and touched and moved daughters more than sons. This same kind of effect was present during feeding: fathers made more frequent attempts to stimulate feeding by moving the bottle for their sons than for their daughters. Mothers appeared to compensate by stimulating their daughter's feeding more than their sons'. The picture is more complicated than this, however. For example, fathers do not hold their sons close and snugly — they reserve this type of holding for their daughters. Mothers, in contrast, tend to hold their sons closer than their daughers. In part, these holding patterns can account for the other observations: if you hold your baby too close, active moving, touching, and other stimulation are difficult to manage.

This pattern of father expressing affection for their daughters and stimulating their sons may be the earliest form of sex-role typing. Fathers, as we know from other research, want to encourage the physical and intellectual development of their sons. For daughters, the fathers' aim may be to encourage femininity. As I will discuss in a later chapter, mothers contribute significantly to their girls' intellectual development; the mother's early stimulation of her infant daughter may be an antecedent of later intellectual encouragment.

These patterns appear to persist throughout infancy. Milton Kotelchuck found that fathers play about one-half hour a day longer with one-year-old firstborn sons than with firstborn daughters. In addition, fathers play different kinds of games with boys and girls. Fathers play physical games such as lifting and tossing more with their boy infants than with their girl infants and vocalize more to their girls than to their boys.[36] In part, this differential treatment may relate to fathers' and mothers' early expectations concerning what baby boys and girls are like. Jefferey Rubin and his colleagues found that even before fathers had ever picked up their newborn infants — when they had only looked at them — they rated their sons as firmer, larger featured, better coordinated, more alert, stronger, and hardier, while daughters were rated as softer, finer featured, inattentive, weaker, and more delicate. As Rubin and his colleagues suggest, it appears that sex typing has already begun at birth, when the parents have only minimal information about their infant. Furthermore, "the labels they ascribe to their newborn infant may well affect subsequent . . . parental behavior itself."[37]

These patterns are not restricted to the United States and Britain. An examination of the Israeli kibbutz, a collective agricultural settlement in which infants are reared in group houses rather than in traditional families, provides further information. Jacob and Hava Gewirtz recorded the visiting patterns of parents and noted how long they stayed when they came to the infant group house for a visit with their sons or daughters. Fathers of infant sons visited longer than fathers of infant daughters. Other evidence provided by anthropologists Mary West and Melvin Konner suggests that these effects may be present in nonmodern cultures as well. In the Kung San of Botswana, a hunting and gathering culture, fathers also spend more time with boys than girls, especially as the infants get older.[38]

Nonhuman primates show this pattern too. Recent laboratory studies show clear differences in the reactions of adult males to male and female infants. Among rhesus monkeys, studied by

William Redican, "mothers tended to play with female infants whereas adult males did so with male infants. In general mothers interacted more positively with female infants and adult males with male infants."[39]

Across cultures, species, and infants of various ages, the sex of the infant or young child significantly affects interaction between parent and child. Parents treat boys and girls differently from birth, and this suggests that the sex-typing process (that is, the process of learning the behavior usually considered appropriate for your sex) may begin much earlier than had previously been thought.

Fathers are interacting much more with their infants than in the past, but many of the traditional role divisions between mothers and fathers remain. Generally, mothers care for babies more than fathers, who in turn spend more of their time with their babies in play. However, both parents contribute to both caregiving and play, although they contribute in different ways. No single profile of the relationship between father and baby does justice to all fathers. Fathers can and do play a significant role in infancy, but how and how much individual fathers influence their infants varies considerably from one family to another.

4 / Socialization and Sociability

Babies begin very early to develop the skills they need for interacting successfully with other people. Sociability begins at home, in the context of the family. Rudolph Schaffer has described three basic steps in the development of social behavior in the first year of life:

> The infant's initial attraction to other human beings that makes him prefer them to inanimate features of the environment.
>
> His learning to distinguish among different human beings so that he can recognize his mother as familiar and strangers as unfamiliar.
>
> His ability, finally, to form a lasting, emotionally meaningful bond with certain specific individuals whose company he actively seeks and whose attention he craves, though he rejects the company and attention of other, strange individuals.[1]

Recent evidence indicates that infants can recognize their mothers by smell even in the first week of life. Moreover, infants can distinguish their parents from strangers by sight by two months and their mothers from their fathers soon thereafter.[2]

The next milestone is the development of a preference for a small number of individuals. Often labeled "attachment," this special desire to be near certain persons and to try to keep them from leaving usually occurs at around seven or eights months of age. Traditional theorists of social development, including both

47

Freud and Bowlby, believed fathers to be less important attachment figures than mothers. In fact, they considered mothers the primary objects of attachment, and there was considerable doubt that infants could initially form attachments to more than one person. The question of whether a baby can form an attachment to its father has fascinated researchers in recent years, and their findings contradict the traditional view.

In the mid-1960s, Rudolph Schaffer and Peggy Emerson published a report entitled "The Development of Social Attachments in Infancy," which challenged the Freud and Bowlby tradition.[3] In their study of 6- to 18-month-old infants in Scotland, Schaffer and Emerson used the amount of protest when the infant was separated from a familiar adult as their measure of attachment. They asked mothers whether their infants cried or fussed when left in their crib, outside a shop in their carriage, or in a room by themselves. Young infants did tend to protest more when mother left than when father did, but this tendency was short-lived. By 18 months, most infants protested the departure of father and mother equally. Moreover, in spite of Freud's emphasis on the importance of the feeding context for the development of attachment, these investigators found that infants developed attachments to a wide range of people—many of whom never participated in routine caretaking activities such as feeding and diapering. Even for mother, the amount of time spent in feeding was not related to the intensity of the infant's attachment. Although feeding appeared not to be critical, Schaffer and Emerson did find that some childrearing behaviors were associated with the infant's attachment. Social stimulation—talking, touching, and playing—was important, as was the adult's responsiveness to the infant's behavior. The adult who responded quickly and reliably when the infant smiled or cried was preferred over less attentive adults. Fathers, of course, are potentially as capable as mothers of stimulating babies and responding to their signals, and thus both fathers and mothers can provide important ingredients for early social development.

Frank Pederson and Kenneth Robson, in the United States, used a different approach but came to a similar conclusion.[4]

They simply asked mothers how their infants responded when fathers returned home from work. The warm and friendly greetings that the majority of 8-month-old infants showed their fathers were viewed as further evidence of infant-father attachment.

Verbal reports, of course, are often unreliable. Later investigators directly observed babies and fathers either in the lab or at home. These observational studies provide a better test of whether attachment between infant and father occurs and how father and mother compare as attachment figures for their young babies. Milton Kotelchuck made some important progress in unraveling this puzzle.[5] In a laboratory playroom he compared infants' reactions to the presence, departure, and return of mother, father, and a stranger. Kotelchuck measured a variety of baby behaviors such as playing, crying, touching, talking, smiling, and how closely the baby stayed to a person or to the door. Let's look at a familiar measure — crying when an adult leaves. Infants 12 months and older tended to cry when either mother and father departed. The difference between their reactions to mother's and father's leaving was very small, suggesting that the 12-month-olds had developed attachments to *both* mother and father. Crying never increased when the stranger left, and the older babies even cried less after the stranger had gone. Other measures tell a similar story. The infants stayed near the door when either parent left, and touched both mother and father when they came back into the room. Neither of these reactions was seen when the stranger left and returned.

Do infants show attachment for both fathers and mothers in the more relaxed and familiar context of the home? Michael Lamb's observation of 7- to 13-month-olds provides an answer.[6] When observed at home, infants reacted to naturally occurring separations from their fathers in the same way as to separations from their mothers. Nor were there any clear preferences for one parent over the other. The babies touched, fussed to, asked to be held by, and sought to be near fathers and mothers to about the same extent.

Some lab studies do indicate that infants prefer to stay near their mothers more than their fathers when both parents are available. How can this finding be reconciled with the earlier claim that infants show no preference between mother and father? The answer lies in the kind of setting in which the observations are made. If the setting is a relaxed or familiar situation, either parent will suffice as an attachment figure. As noted earlier, however, mothers and fathers appear to play different roles. Mothers are more often the primary caregivers, and babies who are hungry, wet, fatigued, or sick are more likely to seek out their mother than their father. Therefore, it is not surprising that infants look to their mothers for comfort in stressful or upsetting situations. Fathers, by contrast, are more likely to be sought out for play. This more complex picture is more satisfactory. Both mother and father are important attachment objects for their infants, but the circumstances that lead to selecting mom or dad may differ.

INDIVIDUAL DIFFERENCES IN FATHERING

All of us know some men who are very involved with their infants and others who are aloof and distant, leaving most of the interaction to their wives. Here are two contrasting fathers:

Warren and Betty K. are sitting in the living room of their apartment when Roger, their 8-month-old, stirs from his nap and begins to cry. Warren ignores the cries and buries himself deeper in his newspaper. Betty leaves the room, and a few moments later she returns with a quieted Roger nuzzling his head on her shoulder. Warren looks up, nods briefly, and goes back to the sports page.

Jim P. is cradling his 4-month-old daughter, Judy, in his arms. He gently strokes her cheek to keep her sucking on the bottle of milk that he is feeding her. A short while later, he sings quietly to Judy and covers her up in her crib. His wife is out for an evening class at the local university. Jim P. does this three nights a week and loves the time alone with his daughter.

Do the different patterns of interaction shown by Warren K.

and Jim P. have different effects on their babies? Let's return briefly to the studies of children's reactions to being left alone with a stranger. In addition to observing parents in the playroom, Kotelchuck interviewed the parents to find out how much time they spent with their babies, and what kind of things they did together with their infants. The infants who interacted least with their fathers in the laboratory had fathers who were least involved in caretaking at home. In fact, there was a positive relationship between the level of paternal caretaking and the amount of time that the infant stayed close to his father in the laboratory. In one study in this series, the investigator even found a positive relationship between how close the infant stayed to his father and the number of diapers changed by the father per week.

It is not only the father's involvement in caretaking that matters. Pedersen and Robson found that besides frequency of the father's caretaking, the intensity of the play interactions between father and infant was important for forming infant-father attachment. Recall that these investigators measured attachment by mother's description of the infant's greeting when father returned from work. However, these factors related only to the level of attachment for boys; there was no clear relationship between the father's behavior and attachment between girl babies and their fathers. This sex difference is not an isolated finding. Other researchers also report that boys, particularly in the second year, show a preference for father over mother.

A word of caution is in order. Although I have discussed these patterns as suggesting that fathers who are more involved *cause* their children to become attached to them, the reverse interpretation cannot be discounted. Perhaps some infants are more inviting, appealing, or interesting. Babies differ in many ways that may affect how involved their parents—both fathers and mothers—will become. In my own research I have found that fathers treat attractive and unattractive babies differently even in the newborn period.[7] Fathers stimulate attractive infants more than less attractive infants; they touch, kiss, and move highly attractive infants more frequently. Differences in the baby's temperament could have an important effect on a burgeoning relationship between father and infant. If a baby is fussy, irritable, and unresponsive in the first few months, perhaps the father will "turn off" and initiate interaction less often. Recent studies in both Sweden and the United States suggest that fathers do respond to temperament differences in babies, but that their reactions depend on the sex of the baby.[8] Fathers are apparently more willing to persist in their interaction with difficult boy babies than with difficult girls. Clearly, the baby's own characteristics can affect the development of the baby's relationship with its father.

Many questions remain to be answered. For example, we do not know how much interaction is needed for infants to develop attachment to their fathers. We need to know much more about the kinds of interactions between fathers and their infants that are most important for the development of the infant's attachment to its father. What role does the mother play in promoting a healthy relationship between father and baby? Researchers will be looking for answers to these questions in future studies.

FROM HOME TO THE OUTSIDE WORLD

As the child gets older it must learn to interact with people outside the family. New adults such as grandparents, aunts and uncles, neighbors, teachers, and store clerks enter the child's world, and the child gets acquainted with other children as well. Developing social skills to interact successfully with new people is an important step for the infant and child. What role do fathers play in helping the child to develop social competence? Does the quality of the early relationship between father and infant affect how well the child can cope with strange adults or with new peers? Can fathers help children to have more fun or more friends?

Very early, even before the infant has developed specific attachments to his father and mother, the quality of the relationship between father and baby seems to affect the baby's social interactions with other adults—perhaps especially if the baby is a boy. Frank Pedersen and his associates tested the reactions of 5-month-old infants to a strange but friendly adult.[9] Even at this young age fathers made a difference to their sons: the 5-month-old boys who had more contact with their fathers were friendlier to the strange adult. They vocalized more at the examiner, showed more readiness to be picked up, and enjoyed frolic play more than baby boys who had less involved fathers. Baby girls, however, did not show such an effect.

These findings, of course, do not mean that fathers ignore their infant daughters, or that fathers have no effect on the development of their girls' social skills. Perhaps fathers influence their girls indirectly by encouraging mother-daughter interaction, or perhaps, as we will see later in this chapter, fathers' influence is more evident when their daughters are older.

As children grow older, fathers continue to contribute to their ability to cope with strangers and strange situations. In the same laboratory study described earlier, Kotelchuck and his colleagues investigated how well the one-year-old infant can cope when left alone with a stranger. They compared three groups of infants — one group with very involved fathers, another with indifferent and uninvolved fathers, and the third with fathers who fell between these extremes. In these infants the most distress occurred in infants with the lowest paternal involvement, an intermediate amount of distress in infants with medium paternal involvement, and the least distress in the infants with highest paternal involvement. It seems that babies who have more contact with their fathers are better able to handle strange situations.

In a related study, Kotelchuck discovered that the less frequently fathers bathed and dressed their infants at home, the longer the infants cried when left alone with a stranger. In short, children whose fathers are active caretakers are better able to handle the stress of being left alone with a stranger. It is possible that more egalitarian families not only share caretaking more but also expose the infant more to other adults, making the infant less likely to be frightened of a strange adult. Also, babies whose parents share child care get used to having one parent leave and be replaced by the other parent. Becoming familiar, in this way, with parental departures may make those babies less afraid of separation from an early age.

K. Alison Clarke-Stewart recently showed that fathers (and mothers) are still affecting children's reactions to unfamiliar adults at 20 months of age.[10] She evaluated the reactions of toddlers to a friendly but unfamiliar woman who interacted with the child in specified ways that included looking, smiling, talking, approaching, playing with a toy, and playing a physical-social game. In contrast to early infancy, *both* boys' and girls' social reactions to the stranger were affected by both their fathers and mothers, but in different ways. When mothers were affectionate and responsive and fathers were available and talkative, girls showed friendly reactions to the strangers. In contrast, boys with an affectionate and responsive mother in combination with a negative or even punitive father were particularly friendly to the female stranger. Perhaps, as Clarke-Stewart suggests, the contrast between an affectionate mother and a punitive father may have made the boys more responsive to women in general. These findings suggest that fathers and mothers may not be interchangeable but may influence their boys' and girls' social development through different kinds of behavior.

These findings are not limited to American children. In some countries fathers have very limited contact with babies. Do these variations in the father's participation affect the infant's ability to cope with strangers? In Guatemala, where paternal caretaking is extremely low, infants protest when left with a stranger at 9 months of age — 3 months ahead of their U.S. counterparts. In Uganda, where fathers also have little to do with infants, infant distress in the presence of a stranger occurs even earlier, at 6 months. These infants behave much like the American infants whose fathers interacted with them least in the Kotelchuck study. However, the father's level of involvement is probably not the only factor that accounts for these cross-cultural patterns; maternal interaction patterns probably vary from culture to culture as well.

Recent evidence gathered by Mary Main and Donna Weston

suggests that the relationships that the infant has developed with *both* mother and father are a better basis for understanding children's social reactions than either the mother-infant or father-infant relationship alone.[11] Main and Weston observed one-year-old infants exploring unfamiliar surroundings in the presence of the mother, the father, and a stranger. Some of the infants appeared comfortable in the strange surroundings when either the mother or father was present, became reasonably upset when either parent left the room, and were happy when either parent returned. Another researcher, Mary Ainsworth, has characterized these infants as "securely attached."[12] Other infants did not seem to get upset when their parents left the room. Furthermore, when parents then returned to the room, these babies showed ambivalence, sometimes approaching them and at other times showing little interest or even angrily pushing their parents away. Ainsworth has termed these infants "insecurely attached." Main and Weston observed two other types of relationships as well, in which babies were securely attached to mother and insecurely attached to father or vice-versa. Even very young children often develop distinctly different relationships with their mothers and fathers. To determine whether the infants' relationships with their mothers and fathers affected their social responsiveness to others, Main and Weston also observed the infants' reactions to a friendly clown. The infants who were securely attached to both parents were more responsive to the clown than those who were securely attached to only one parent and insecurely attached to the other, and the babies who were insecurely attached to both parents were the least sociable with the clown. These results suggest that a less than optimal relationship with one parent can be compensated for by a better relationship with the other parent — and therefore that it is not enough to study just fathers. Viewing the father as part of a family system is the best way of understanding his role in child development.

FATHERS, PEERS, AND POPULARITY

It is not known whether a father's relationship with his infant affects the infant's (or the older child's) ability to make friends.

Everett Waters and his colleagues have found that toddlers who have already formed a good relationship with their mothers get along better with a new peer.[13] Since fathers are so important as play partners, it is highly likely that the father-infant relationship does affect the child's emerging relationships with peers.

Studies of older boys whose fathers are absent suggests that fathers do indeed affect how well children are accepted by their peers. Lois Stolz studied children who were infants during World War II, when many of their fathers were away at war. When the children were 4 to 8 years old, Stolz found that the ones whose fathers had been absent during their infancy had poorer peer relationships. Studies of the sons of Norwegian sailors, who are away for many months at a time, point to the same conclusion: the boys whose fathers are often absent are less popular and have less satisfying peer-group relationships than boys whose fathers are regularly available.[14] But why? Possibly boys who grow up without their fathers have less chance to learn the behavior that other boys in our culture value. Perhaps, for example, they tend to be shy, timid, and reluctant to play rough games — traits that may not always make a boy popular with his peers.

FATHERS AND SEX-ROLE DEVELOPMENT

Fathers have an important effect on children's sex-role development. In Chapter 3 we have already seen the early beginnings of this influence. Recall that even when the baby is still in the hospital, fathers, especially, treat their boys and girls differently, and that later fathers play in different ways with their sons and daughters. Fathers, even more than mothers, seem to play a critical role in children's developing sex-role behaviors.

It is important to remember that sex roles for boys and girls, just as for men and women, are in a state of flux. Although stereotypes concerning the "right" behaviors for boys and girls still exist, many adults and children today have less rigid views of how boys and girls ought to act. Many of the research findings show "differences" in behavior that deviate from these stereotypes, but they are just that — differences — and not necessarily deficits or problems. It is important to remember this caveat as I review some of the sex-typing literature.

One of the most common research strategies in this area has been to examine how children develop in homes where no father is present. If fathers play a crucial part in teaching children sex-roles, children from homes in which the father is permanently absent or away for long periods might show disruptions in sex-typing. Single-parent families are no longer uncommon. A majority of American children will live in a household with only one parent at some point during their growing years. What is the effect of this situation on children's learning of sex roles? Differences in sex-role typing in children from father-present and father-absent homes are most often found in preadolescent boys. However, these differences depend on how old the boy is when his father leaves. To determine the importance of age of separation, Mavis Hetherington trained male supervisors in a recreation center to observe the behavior of two groups of boys:[15] one group who had been 6 years old or older when their fathers left, and one group whose fathers had left before they were 5 years old. The two groups behaved very differently. Boys who had been separated from their fathers before the age of 5 were more dependent on their peers and less assertive. They played fewer rough physical contact sports such as football, boxing, or soccer. Instead they chose reading, drawing, or working on puzzles — nonphysical and noncompetitive activities. In contrast, if the father was available until 6 years of age, his later departure didn't have this effect. Boys whose fathers left when they were 6 or older behaved in these areas the same as boys raised in intact homes. Although both groups of boys were showing acceptable patterns of behavior, the father-absent boys were simply exhibiting behaviors that were not stereotypically "masculine."

The effects of father's absence on older boys are less clear. Some investigators find no differences between "father absent" and "father present" boys. Others find a pattern called "compensatory masculinity" in boys separated from their fathers. In this pattern the boy sometimes displays excessive "masculine" bravado and at other times shows "feminine" behavior such as dependency. Delinquents are often found to have this combination of flamboyant swaggering toughness and sexuality and at the same time dependent behaviors. This may be accounted for by the high rates of father's absence found in homes of delinquent children.[16] One reason for the decreasing effect of father's absence in older boys is that as boys grow up they encounter a host of other masculine models — teachers, peers, siblings, surrogate fathers, and even TV heroes. Many of the lessons in masculinity that they can't learn from their fathers are learned later from these other models. Even an older brother can be such a model: in families without fathers, boys who have older brothers show more traditionally masculine behavior patterns than boys without big brothers.[17]

Just as in the case of boys, father's absence can be disruptive to the sex-typing of girls. The most striking evidence of this comes from Mavis Hetherington. She reasoned that earlier studies showed no effects of father absence on girls because they measured the wrong behaviors at the wrong time. According to Marion Johnson's theory of reciprocal role-taking, fathers are particularly important for helping girls learn to interact with males. In our culture, this generally doesn't begin until adolescence. So in contrast to the earlier studies that examined the behavior of preadolescent girls, Hetherington studied adolescent girls.[18]

Hetherington compared girls who lived with both parents with girls who lived only with their mothers (due to divorce or the death of their father) on a number of traditional measures (for example, the extent of their "feminine" interests, activities, and behaviors) as well as on some less traditional measures (for example, interaction with males). She found that although the groups of girls were, to a large extent, similar in their interests, activities, and behavior, they differed somewhat in their behavior with males. Both groups of fatherless girls reported feeling anxious around males, but the two groups had apparently developed different ways of coping with this anxiety. Daughters of widows appeared shy and uncomfortable when around males, in contrast to daughters of divorced mothers who were much more assertive with male peers and men, both initiating and responding more to them, than either the daughters of widows or the girls from intact families. For example, when the girls were observed at a dance, the daughters of widows stayed with the other girls and frequently hid behind other girls. Some even spent most of the evening hiding in the ladies' room. The daughters of the divorcees behaved very differently, spending more time at the boys' end of the hall, more often initiating encounters, and asking male peers to dance. How do we account for these patterns? All of the mothers were equally "feminine" and reinforced their daughters for sex-appropriate behaviors. Hetherington suggests that daughters of divorced women may have viewed their mothers' lives as unsatisfying and felt that for happiness it was essential to secure a man. In contrast, daughters of widows may have idealized their fathers and felt that few other men could compare favorably with them, or alternatively may have regarded all men as superior and as objects of deference and apprehension.

A word of caution: the fatherless girls in this study came from rather extreme and unusual samples. No other males were in the house — either brothers or stepfathers. These girls were deprived of contacts with males in general — not just fathers. As divorce becomes increasingly common and, along with it, the rate of remarriage increases, such girls may show less extreme reactions. Also, mothers may react less negatively to divorce today than they did in the 1960s, when Hetherington conducted her study. Attitudes toward marriage and divorce continue to change with the times.

Studying children whose father are absent is not the only way to study fathers' effect on children's sex-typing, and it may not be the best way. Families without fathers may differ from intact nuclear families in many ways, and therefore it is often difficult to tell whether the differences between children from these two types of families are caused *only* by the father's absence. Pedersen has summarized this problem:

> Children growing up in a single-parent home headed by the mother may be affected by any of the following: the altered family structure and consequent differences in maternal role behav-

ior; the child's diminished or changed quality of interaction with a male adult; proportionally greater interaction with the mother; the presence of surrogate caregivers associated with the mother's employment; or qualitatively different maternal behavior vis-à-vis the child because of the emotional meaning the father's absence has to her. There are many others factors which also may operate either singly or in concert with each other, allowing absolutely no possibility for delineating the "true" causal agents on the child's development.[19]

Because of these problems, researchers have turned to other ways of investigating the father's role in sex-typing, such as by studying the father's influence in intact families, particularly the influence of variations in the ways individual fathers interact with their boys and girls. Are fathers warm, supportive, or hostile? Do they encourage their children to use them as role models? Parental warmth and nurturance are particularly important in sex-typing; a number of researchers over the past two decades have found that when the same-sex parent is warm and supportive, learning of sex-role behaviors traditionally viewed as appropriate for boys and girls is enhanced. However, whereas both maternal and paternal warmth increase femininity in girls, paternal but not maternal warmth is associated with high traditional masculinity in boys, according to Hetherington. And, of course, the relationship between mother and father is also important. Sex-typing of boys, especially, is affected by whether mother or father is more powerful in family decisionmaking. In families where mothers generally make decisions while fathers are more passive, boys are less likely to use their fathers as role models. As a result, they exhibit fewer traditionally defined masculine behaviors. Boys who fit the masculine stereotype have fathers who are decisive and dominant in setting limits, and who play an active role in disciplining their sons. These variations in the division of parental power do not seem to affect the development of traditionally defined feminine characteristics in girls.[20]

Fathers also affect the sex-typing of their daughters, but in different ways from the ways they affect boys. Femininity in daughters is related to father's masculinity, father's approval of the mother as a model for his daughter, and father's encouragement of his daughter's participation in feminine activities. And the father's influence does not end in early childhood. Even in adolescence and adulthood, the daughters' relationships with males are more influenced by their earlier relations with their fathers than by their relations with their mothers. Fathers who are aloof, uninvolved, or hostile have been linked with problems for women in forming lasting heterosexual relationships.[21]

More recently researchers have relied on more direct observations of interaction between fathers and children. One strategy is to set up situations where fathers' reactions to children's sex-role choices can be observed. Using this approach, Judith Langlois recently found that fathers enforce sex-role standards even in play situations. Not only do fathers choose different kinds of toys for boys and girls, but they encourage play that they consider sex-appropriate and discourage types of play that they consider sex-inappropriate. Langlois found that this is more true of fathers than of mothers.[22] She observed 3- and 5-year-old boys and girls with their fathers in a laboratory playroom that included a carefully chosen set of toys that were traditionally considered appropriate for either boys or girls. The fathers' reaction to their children's play was recorded under two conditions: when the sex-appropriate toys were available and when only sex-inappropriate toys were present. Do fathers react differently when their sons play with toy soldiers and cars from when they play with pots and pans and doll furniture? And do they behave in the same way when their daughter plays cowboy as when she plays nurse? Fathers in this study reacted very differently depending on the traditional sex-role appropriateness of the toys. They rewarded their children — by approving, helping, and joining in the play — more often for play with sex-appropriate toys than for play with sex-inappropriate toys, and they discouraged play with sex-inappropriate toys more than play with sex-appropriate toys. Moreover, fathers were generally more positive to their girls than to their boys and more punitive to their boys than to their girls. Boys who played with the "feminine" toys (doll furniture, pots and pans) received the lowest amount of reward from their fathers.

In a similar study, Langlois investigated the role that mothers and peers play in teaching children their sex roles. Just as in the earlier study, she observed the reactions of mothers and peers to children's play with sex-typed toys in a laboratory playroom. Mother and peers behaved very differently not only from the fathers in the earlier study but also from each other. Mothers encouraged both boys and girls to play with toys traditionally considered appropriate for girls. At the same time, mothers tended to punish both their boys and their girls for playing with "masculine" toys. Peers, who were generally less rewarding than mothers, reacted much the way fathers did, encouraging both boys and girls to play with sex-appropriate toys and actively punishing play with toys considered appropriate for the opposite sex, especially among boys. When boys played with dolls, their peers often interrupted by hitting and ridiculing. Langlois's findings indicate that children learn how persons of their sex are expected to act from a variety of social agents, not just from fathers. But the findings also underscore the more discriminating role of fathers — in contrast to mothers — in sex-typing.

Another way in which fathers may contribute to their children's learning of sex roles is by the way they treat their children's privacy. Douglas Sawin and I have found that fathers respect their daughters' privacy more than that of their sons; fathers of daughters, especially when their girls reach adolescence, are more likely to knock before entering their daughter's bedroom. Mothers, by contrast, knock less than fathers and appear to make little distinction between sons and daughters in their knocking on bedroom doors.[23] Again, fathers discriminate between boys and girls more than mothers do.

Fathers, then, influence the process of sex-typing in a myriad of ways — through their personalities, by serving as role models, and in their daily interactions with their children. Even more than mothers, they have a striking impact on the development of sex-typed behavior in their boys and girls. Families vary enormously in their organization, their values, and their aspirations for their children, and the particular characteristics that sons and daughters display will depend, in the final analysis, on all of these factors. As our concepts of what behavior is appropriate for boys and girls shift, so may the father's role in this process. Whatever his role in the future, if the past is a reliable guide, it is likely to be a major one.

5/Intellectual Development

What determines a person's intelligence? This question has aroused debate for years, and the controversy shows no signs of dying down. Most experts recognize the contribution of genetics to intelligence, but stress the importance of a variety of environmental influences in shaping children's intellectual development. How do fathers, as one of the environmental factors that influence children's intelligence, contribute to their children's intellectual growth? Fathers can affect how well their children progress in school, which subjects they prefer, and even the kinds of occupations they choose. Whether a child prefers reading and hates math or aspires to be a physicist or an engineer rather than a book critic or a historian is clearly affected by the father's attitudes, encouragement, and behavior.

EARLY INFLUENCES

Both fathers and mothers can influence their infant's mental development. One important way is through direct stimulation—touching, talking, and playing. Numerous studies have shown that babies need social stimulation if they are to make adequate cognitive progress. The role of stimulation is dramatically illustrated by classic studies of infants raised in foundling homes or orphanages. Often, in the interests of hygiene, babies were kept in separate cubicles. They had only brief, hurried contacts with adults when they were cleaned or fed. This unstimulating early environment was disastrous for the babies' mental growth: many of them became severely mentally retarded.

Even in a normal home environment, variations in the type and amount of stimulation can affect an infant's intellectual development. Leon Yarrow, Judy Rubinstein, and Frank Pedersen found that the amount and variety of social stimulation — rocking, talking, looking, touching — that 5-month-old infants received was positively related to their level of mental ability. And, just as I noted in the earlier discussion of the development of social responsiveness in babies, the timing of the talking, touching, and other stimulation was found to be important. The parents of the intellectually advanced infants stimulated their infants *in response to* an infant signal such as a smile or a cry. Adult stimulation is most effective when it is not random, but contingent upon or responsive to the behavior of the infant. As Yarrow and his colleagues put it:

> It is likely that response to an infant's cries does more than reinforce crying. It reinforces active coping with the environment, reaching out to obtain feedback from people and objects. Moreover, in time, an infant whose parent is quickly responsive to his cries may come to feel that through his own actions he can have an effect on other people and his environment.[1]

From these early exchanges between baby and parents, the infant learns an important lesson: "I can affect other people through my own actions."

As I noted in Chapter 3, infants may acquire a general belief about whether or not they can have an effect on people and events in their enviornment very early in life. This belief not only is important in infancy but continues to be an important determinant of both cognitive and social progress throughout childhood. For example, children who believe their success in spelling or math is due to their own efforts rather than to luck or some other external factor, such as a nasty teacher, often achieve more and persist longer in the face of failure.[2] It may be that these later differences have their early antecedents in infancy.

Moreover, these findings illustrate the bidirectional nature of children's cognitive development: by their behaviors infants and children affect parents' behaviors, just as parents influence them.

Fathers clearly provide the kinds of experiences for their infants that promote cognitive growth, and their impact begins at a much earlier age than anyone had imagined until recently. According to Pedersen, Rubinstein, and Yarrow, this influence begins as early as 5 to 6 months of age. One way to demonstrate that father's input is helpful to the infant's cognitive progress is to compare infants whose fathers live with them with infants whose fathers are absent. Pedersen and his colleagues made such a comparison using the Bayley Scales of Infant Development — a measure of infant cognitive status — and found that boy babies whose fathers were absent got lower scores.[3] At the age of 5 or 6 months, the Bayley scales measure sensory-motor behaviors such as reaching, grasping, and following an object, which are thought to be precursors of later intellectual development. For girl babies, the presence or absence of father made no difference on any of these measures of cognitive development. Another early indication of cognitive progress is how much interest babies show in things and events in their environment. Researchers have found that this early form of curiosity is also related to later intellectual development. Pedersen and his colleagues gave the infants a new and unfamiliar toy and recorded how much time they spent manipulating and exploring it. The boy babies who were living without fathers spent less time examining the strange object than those with live-in fathers.

It is not simply the presence or absence of a father in the home that makes a difference to boys' intellectual development. The amount of stimulation that live-in fathers provide their infant sons is important as well. Baby boys who have more frequent contact with their fathers score higher on the cognitive development measures. For infant girls, neither father's absence nor how involved the live-in fathers are seems to affect cognitive progress — at least in early infancy. Fathers do influence their daughters' intellectual growth, but not until later in their development.

These studies of children whose fathers are absent are often difficult to interpret, as was discussed in Chapter 4. Perhaps there are fewer adults present in homes without fathers, and the infants simply receive less total intellectual stimulation because one parent alone cannot possibly spend as much time with the child as two parents can. Fortunately, Pedersen and his colleagues checked and found that there were an equal number of adults in the father-absent and father-present households in their study. Father, it seems, is not just another adult but appears to have "an impact that is qualitatively different from other adults."[4]

Other investigators provide clues concerning behaviors through which fathers contribute to their infants' cognitive growth. K. Alison Clarke-Stewart suggests that fathers and mothers both help the infant develop intellectually, but in different ways: the father through his physical skill as a playmate and the mother through her verbal and teaching talents.[5]

Clarke-Stewart observed infants when they were 15, 20, and 30 months of age. To assess "natural" or spontaneous behavior at home, she conducted a series of one-hour observations at each age — when mother was alone with the infant and when mother, father, and infant were together. She kept track of parental behavior previously found to relate to children's cognitive development, such as talking, touching, and playing, as well as the level of parental responsiveness. How responsive a parent is to the child's social initiations — a smile, a kiss, showing, or giving — is an important influence on the child's intellectual and language development. Parents were asked to choose among different games that they could play with their child. Some were social/physical activities (such as having a pretend tea party, brushing the child's hair, playing "this little piggy"), while others were intellectually stimulating games (reading a story, playing with a stacking toy, building with blocks), and still others were games that the child could play alone. Clarke-Stewart hoped to find differences in the activities that parents prefer and to see if parental preferences relate to how the child develops cognitively. Are some parents more skillful playmates than others?

To find out, she asked the parents to play a series of specific games — to see whether mothers and fathers differed as playmates. The games ranged from coloring and making designs with drinking straws to blowing bubbles and throwing and rolling a ball. Finally, she asked parents to indicate at what age they expected that their child would be able to do certain tasks, such as going next door alone, using a hammer, crossing the street, playing with scissors, or taking a bath without help. Training for independence has been found by other investigators to relate to children's achievement levels.

Clarke-Stewart probed the child's intellectual and social competence using the Bayley Scales of Infant Development at 16 and 22 months, and using a closely related measure of cognitive development that is more suitable for 30-month-old children at the final testing point. These test situations in combination with the natural observations suggest a great deal about the ways mothers and fathers influence their children's early intellectual development. The most important finding was that mothers and fathers contributed in different ways to their infant's cognitive advancement.

A number of types of behavior by mothers seemed to help infants develop cognitively. Stimulating their infants by talking and showing and demonstrating toys was one effective way. Others were the expression of warmth and affection, and an emphasis on intellectual acceleration — as measured by the mothers' choice of intellectual activities, such as reading. In short, verbal and toy stimulation in combination with affection appear to be the important things that mothers do in helping their infants develop cognitive skills. In earlier work, Clarke-Stewart found this same set of maternal behaviors to be related to infant language and cognitive development. She described this pattern as "optimal maternal care."

Optimal paternal care, however, seems to be different; fathers influenced their young children's cognitive progress in other ways. The father's skill as a playmate was one of the main predictors of children's cognitive development. Fathers who were good at peek-a-boo, ball toss, and bouncing bouts had more cognitively advanced children than those who couldn't keep their children interested in their games. A second contributor was the father's anticipation of the child's independence. How early the father expected his child to be able to handle a pair of scissors or take a bath alone was positively related to the child's cognitive development.

We saw earlier that fathers affected the cognitive development of young male infants but not of young female infants. In older infants and children, however, Clarke-Stewart found that both boys and girls are affected by fathers — as well as by mothers. However, fathers and mothers influence their sons and daughters in different ways. A father's prowess as a playmate — particularly at physically stimulating play — relates to boys' intellectual development more than to that of girls. In contrast, fathers affected their daughters' cognitive progress through verbal stimulation such as talking, praising, and complimenting and through being responsive to their daughters' social initiatives. Mothers influenced their daughters mainly through verbal and intellectual stimulation; in contrast, mothers affected their sons' cognitive development mainly through physical contacts in social play and through social responsiveness. The pattern is complex but clear: both mother and fathers influence girls through verbal interaction and warmth and boys through physical interaction. It is clear that fathers and mothers both play influential, but distinctive, roles in encouraging the cognitive development of their infants and young children. And the effects are detected very early in life. Which specific cognitive skills are affected most by fathers, which by mothers, and when these different effects occur remains to be discovered.

Parents influence their infants not only through direct interaction but also by the ways they organize their infants' environment. For example, the number, type, and variety of toys that parents make available is one way they "manage" their children's environment. Parents set boundaries as well: they limit the areas in the home in which the infant can explore. Being too restrictive can hamper infants' cognitive growth; giving infants the freedom to explore their environment visually and physically can enhance their mental development.

One psychologist, Burton White, has made the case very strongly:

> the effective child-rearer makes the living area as safe as possible for the naive newly crawling or walking child and then provides maximum access to the living area for the child. This immediately sets the process of development off in a manner that will lead naturally to the satisfaction of and the further development of the child's curiosity; the opportunity to learn much about the world at large; and the opportunity to enter into natural useful relationships with people. The child-rearer not only provides maximum access to the living area, but in addition he or she makes kitchen cabinets attractive and available and then keeps a few materials in reserve for those times when the child may become a bit bored.[6]

Fathers and mothers differ in how much exploratory freedom they encourage: fathers tend to allow their infants to explore, while mothers are more cautious and tend to put stricter limits on exploration. This pattern is not limited to infancy. As the child develops, fathers generally encourage independent, exploratory behavior more than mothers—both inside and outside the home. Boys, especially, are likely to be trained to be independent and exploratory. Boys are allowed to cross the street alone earlier, to stay away from home more, and to explore a wider area of their neighborhood than are girls. And these opportunities may make a difference. As one researcher puts it, "The boys' experience in these independent explorations, which girls lack, very likely has considerable importance in the development of independent coping styles, a sense of competence, and even specific skills."[7] Fathers in particular are likely to provide these important opportunities for their developing boys.

BEYOND INFANCY

The impact of fathers on their children's intellectual development does not end with infancy. Studies of older children have followed the same two approaches as studies of infants: examining the effect of father's absence on the child's development and directly observing the effect of fathers on their children's cognitive development. One finding is clear from both of these approaches: just as is true in infancy, fathers affect the cognitive development of both boys and girls, but in different ways.

Fathers' absence usually refers to a situation in which the father is permanently absent from the home because of death, divorce, or desertion. However, these are not the only causes of father's absence. Even fathers who are still members of the family may often be unavailable to their children because of schedules, travel, or just lack of interest. In an important study, Robert Blanchard and Henry Biller demonstrated that fathers' availability, as well as fathers' absence, affects children's academic performance. Four groups of third-grade boys were compared; all were of average IQ, were from working-class and middle-class backgrounds, and had the same constellation of siblings. Two groups of boys came from homes without fathers: in one group the father had left before the boy was 5 years old; in the other group, the father had left after the boy's fifth birthday. The other two groups were from intact families, but the amount of time that the fathers typically spent interacting with their sons varied: less than 6 hours per week in one group, more than 2 hours per day or more than 14 hours per week in the other. Both the age at which the father had left and the father's availability made a difference. The underachievers, who were working below grade level, came from homes where the father had left before the child was 5. The superior academic performers were the boys whose fathers were present and highly available. The boys who had lost their fathers after age 5 and those whose fathers were generally unavailable were functioning somewhat below grade level. According to Biller, highly available fathers help their sons reach their intellectual potential.

Highly available fathers can be models of perseverance and achievement motivation. The father can be an example of a male successfully functioning outside of the home atmosphere. Frequent opportunity to observe and imitate an adequate father contributes to the development of the boys' overall instrumental and problem-solving ability. However, having a competent father will not facilitate a boy's intellectual development if the father is not consistently accessible to the boy or if the father-son relationship is negative in quality.[8]

The findings from this study are typical of research using the "father absence" approach to study the effect of fathers on children's intellectual development. It is not only boys who are affected by the lack of a father. Although girls are less often included in such studies, when they are examined, their cognitive development seems to be detrimentally affected by the father's absence as well. Marybeth Shinn, in a recent comprehensive review of the effects of father's absence on children's cognitive development, found considerable differences in cognitive performance between children from intact nuclear families and fatherless families in terms of achievement test scores, IQ scores, and grade-point average.[9]

Why do children from homes without fathers perform poorly in school and on IQ tests? Attention, encouragement, and stimulation affect a child's cognitive development—especially when they come in response to the child's achievements and emerging abilities and skills. One explanation for the lower level of cognitive ability of children from single-parent households may be that these children receive less adult attention and interact less with adults than do children in two-parent families. Divorced mothers are less likely to read to their children at bedtime, to prolong child-care routines in a playful way, or even to eat with their children. In a single-parent household with a number of children, some of the teaching, playing, and caregiving may be taken over by older brothers and sisters. In some African cultures, studied by Herbert and Gloria Leiderman, where siblings and other children give care and stimulation to young children, the level of intellectual growth is lower than in cultures where adults play these roles. Robert Zajonc has offered a similar explanation for why later-born children in large families perform less well on cognitive tasks: their siblings, not their parents, are their teachers.[10] Therefore, it is too simple to attribute these effects entirely to the lack of a father in the home. A better way to evaluate the effect of fathers on intellectual development is to observe father-child interactions directly.

An example of the observational approach is a series of studies of 4-year-olds and their fathers by Norma Radin. She interviewed the father at home while his 4-year-old child was present. The ways the father handled his child's interruptions during the interview were systematically observed and recorded. Did he praise the child? Did he ask the child questions? Did he scold or reprimand? Later the children were given an intelligence test and a vocabulary test. Boys of fathers who were nurturant (kind, praising, helpful) scored higher on the tests than boys of fathers who were nonnurturant (cool, aloof). Similarly, restrictive behavior by fathers was associated with low cognitive scores for boys. For girls, Radin found few consistent relationships between cognitive status and how their fathers acted.[11]

Fathers may affect their daughters indirectly through their wives. In one California study of children between the ages of 21 months and 15 years, Marjorie Honzik found that the father's friendliness toward the mother fostered the intellectual growth of girls. Possibly girls are more likely to adopt their mother as a role model in a family where the father is supportive of his wife; in turn, as Radin puts it, "the daughters' intellectual growth may be stimulated through their emulation of their mothers' problem solving strategies and thinking processes."[12]

Others have shown that fathers do have a direct impact on their daughters' cognitive development, but that it may not always be positive. Fathers, even more than mothers, tend to respond to their children in sex-stereotyped ways and to encourage masculine pursuits in their sons and feminine ones in their daughters. Since intellectual achievement is still viewed by some parents — in spite of recent changes — as a masculine activity, fathers may actually undermine their daughters' intellectual advancement because they view academic success as unfeminine.

This attitude is seen very clearly in situations where mother and father help their child on a problem-solving task or a complex puzzle under the watchful eye of the videotape camera. These observations show that fathers, more than mothers, treat their sons and daughters differently. In one such study, for example, Jeanne Block found that fathers, especially, are likely to discourage their daughters, in subtle ways, from achieving. Instead of focusing on their daughters' performance on the task, fathers seemed more concerned with interpersonal aspects of the situation. They spent more time encouraging, supporting, joking, playing, and protecting their daughters than giving helpful hints on how to do better at the task. With their sons, by contrast, fathers concentrated on performance. They might explain the principles of the task to their sons, and they emphasized mastering the task rather than simply enjoying the game. Fathers set higher standards for their sons as well. And they reacted differently when boys and girls asked for help in solving a problem. They answered task-oriented questions and requests for help from boys more than girls. With girls they tended to give help even when it wasn't requested — thus encouraging daughters to be inappropriately dependent, a tendency that prevails throughout the school years. Both fathers and mothers not only appear to discourage independent achievement in their daughters, but, as Block puts it, may "devalue their daughters as well. Parents interrupt their daughters more than their sons thus conveying a message that the ideas of their daughters are considered less important, less worthy of respect."[13] Boys and girls receive very different messages from their parents, especially their fathers: for boys the message is "do well"; for girls it is "have a good time." And just as we saw in infancy, these experiences are likely to undermine the girl's belief that the world is responsive to her actions. The view that through one's own actions the world can be altered is important for developing persistence and a sense of mastery — important ingredients for success in achievement situations.

This same lesson is reflected in the educational and occupational expectations that parents have for their sons and daughters. Both parents, but especially fathers, are most likely to stress the importance of a career and occupational success for their sons than for their daughters. Everyone can recall being introduced to "Harold, my son the doctor" — who is 6 months old and sleeping at the time. It is rare to be introduced to Sarah, the lawyer, or Janet, the corporation president. There is truth in this anecdote, according to Lois Hoffman, who in 1975 asked more than 2000 mothers and fathers, "What kind of person would you want your son (daughter) to become?"[14] Fathers, even more than mothers, demonstrated the "my son the doctor" syndrome and emphasized occupational success more for their sons than for their daughters. Not only were parents more concerned about career success for their sons, but twice as many parents indicated they wanted their boys to be hardworking and ambitious as opposed to their girls. The other traits that parents desired in their sons, such as being intelligent, self-reliant, responsible, and strong-willed, were all clearly focused on fostering the boys' occupational achievement. There was much less focus on doing well in work and career for girls. Parents hoped their girls would be kind, unselfish, loving, attractive, and well-mannered, would have a good marriage, and would be a good mother. These expectations take their toll on girl's later achievement.

As social values shift, and as more women enter the work force, it is likely that fathers' expectations for their daughters will change and fathers will expect similar levels of achievement from their children — regardless of their sex. In Norma Radin's words, if the father "sets up a relationship in which his daughter can model his intellectual efforts and achievement motivation and be reinforced for doing so, he can heighten these attributes in his daughter."[15] Indeed, there are classic historical examples that illustrate how fathers can enhance their daughters' cognitive and intellectual development. Indira Gandhi, Prime Minister of India, was highly influenced by her father, Jawaharlal Nehru. According to her biographer, M. C. Rau:

> Indira was not educated on conventional lines but the circumstances and personality of her father combined to give her

one of the rarest educations that a person can acquire. Nehru took keen interest in her education and encouraged her to read and think for herself. While he was away, he carried on with the Great Dialogue through letters.[16]

Gandhi is not an isolated example. Consider Margaret Mead. In her autobiography, *Blackberry Winter*, she attributes much of her success and values to her father:

> He taught me the importance of thinking clearly and of keeping one's premises clear . . . It was proper for women to be committed to pure goodness and purely intellectual activities . . . It was my father, even more than my mother, whose career was limited by the number of her children and her health, who defined for me my place in the world.[17]

And there are others as well. Margaret Thatcher, the British Prime Minister, was strongly encouraged in her early years by her father. And so were a number of other women of achievement such as Congresswomen Shirley Chisolm and opera star Beverly Sills. Fathers can positively affect their daughters' cognitive development; often they simply fail to do it!

6 / Divorce and Custody

Divorce has a profound impact on families, producing stresses and changes in fathers, mothers, and children. In both the United States and Great Britain, divorce rates are increasing. The annual divorce rate in the United States doubled between 1965 and 1976. Today about half of all new marriages are likely to end in divorce. In Great Britain the rate tripled between 1967 and 1976, and now about one in five marriages ends in divorce. In the United States 60 percent and in Great Britain nearly 75 percent of the divorces involve children. Although attitudes and laws about child custody are changing, mothers still gain custody of children in 90 percent of divorce cases. In 1979 only 10 percent of children of divorced parents in the United States and 7 percent in Great Britain lived with their fathers—though these proportions had tripled since 1960. Fathers are more likely to get custody of school-age children than of younger children. It is important to realize, however, that even if they do not live with their children, divorced fathers can influence their children's development.

Divorce is often viewed as a single event or a crisis, but this may be too simple. It is more useful to think of it as "a sequence of experiences involving a transition in the lives of children."[1] Often a period of conflict and disagreement among family members precedes the separation. After the separation there is often a lengthy period of disorganization and disruption and at the same time a search for new strategies for handling the new and different life situation. New schedules are being tried out, moves to new homes and neighborhoods often occur, visitation patterns are being established, and new budget tactics are being explored. Eventually a new phase occurs in which the single-parent family settles on a new but stable and organized life style. A variety of factors such as the cause of the divorce, the financial status of the family, the age and sex of the children, the kind of separation settlement, and especially the custody arrangements and the kinds of social support available from relatives, friends, and neighbors can influence how quickly and how successfully families adjust to divorce. Fathers — even though they generally do not gain custody of their children — have a significant effect on the course of divorce.

MATERNAL CUSTODY

One of the most recent and most ambitious studies of divorce in which mother had custody of the children was conducted by Mavis Hetherington and her colleagues.[2] To explore the impact of divorce on how families function, Hetherington studied 96 families over a two-year period. Half of the families were divorced and half were intact families. The children were approximately four years old at the time of the divorce. The families were studied at three time points — two months, one year, and two years after the divorce. Hetherington tried to answer a variety of questions about the impact of divorce: How do the parents fare? How do children manage after a divorce? Does the father affect how well the mother and children manage to cope with divorce?

Divorce may cause psychological upset, but first consider the practical side. Running a household singlehandedly is a lot more difficult than sharing the responsibility with a helpful spouse. In addition to suffering many problems of maintaining a household alone, both mothers and fathers encountered financial problems. As a result of the divorce, they often had to move to new and smaller homes in less desirable neighborhoods, — moves that involved not only loss of friends and neighbors but possibly poorer schools and more crime and threats to personal safety.

The parents' self-concepts suffered: divorced mothers and fathers felt less competent and less able to cope with daily demands. And this problem showed in the degree of household disorganization. Schedules were often missed, meals were often "on the fly" at irregular times, mothers and children ate together less often, bedtime schedules were more erratic, and children were more often late for school. The mothers—who were caring for the children—were more disorganized than the fathers, but fathers suffered disorganization in their lives as well.

In a marriage that works, husband and wife mutually support each other. The removal of this emotional, social, and often economic support through divorce can have serious consequences—at least in the short run—for mothers and fathers as individuals. The divorced parents in Hetherington's study did not fare too well emotionally; in the first year following divorce, they felt more anxious, depressed, and angry than nondivorced parents. The effects were more severe and lasted longer for divorced mothers than for fathers—particularly mothers of boys. Even after two years they were still feeling less competent, more anxious, and angrier than married mothers or mothers of girls.

These practical and emotional disruptions are naturally reflected in the parent-child relationships. Both mothers and fathers are less effective parents after divorce, especially in the first year, although there is a clear pattern of improvement over time. Divorced parents settled for less mature behavior from their children than parents from intact families would accept. The divorced parents expected their children to accept fewer responsibilities—a factor that may have contributed to the household disorganization.

Divorced mothers and fathers differed in how indulgent and friendly they were and how restrictive and negative they acted toward their children. Differences between mothers and fathers are not surprising, since the mothers had continual access to their children as a result of receiving custody and also had continual responsibility, while fathers had limited and less frequent contact with their children. Divorced mothers generally showed less affection toward their children of either sex than did married mothers, and especially toward their sons. Besides being less affectionate, the divorced mothers treated their sons more harshly and gave them more threatening commands — though they did not systematically enforce them. "Divorced mothers were barking out orders like a general in the field, but were not following through and responding appropriately to either their sons' negative or positive behavior." Fathers, on the other hand, tended to treat every day as Christmas and to be permissive and indulgent — a pattern that probably made it even tougher for mothers to control their children. And it showed in the children's behavior — especially the boys'. The boys in divorced families didn't obey or attend to their mothers, but they did whine, nag, and demand. Additionally, they were more aggressive than boys in intact families. As Hetherington notes: "Some desperate divorced mothers described their relationship with their children one year after divorce as 'declared war,' 'a struggle for survival,' 'the old chinese water torture,' or like getting bitten to death by ducks."[3]

The first year after divorce appears to be a particularly difficult period for divorced parents and their children; parents seem to have a tougher time with their children at one year after divorce than at two months after divorce. After two years, the situation was much better, with both parents and children adapting to the situation. Fathers dropped their Santa Claus role and toughened up and became more restrictive with their children, while mothers became less restrictive. Even after two years, however, the boys in the divorced families were still more aggressive, more impulsive, and more disobedient with their mothers than either girls in divorced families or children in intact families. Clearly, boys suffered more than girls as a result of divorce and the accompanying loss of the father as a live-in parent. This finding highlights our earlier observations concerning the particular importance of the father-son relationship.

What happens at home may affect the child's behavior at school, just as conflict at home may disrupt a parent's functioning at work. As I noted in Chapter 4, different social relationships with parents in infancy seem to be associated with making friends in the preschool years. Negative, conflictful relations among family members often spill over and affect a child's relationships with peers.

Hetherington and her colleagues examined the play and social interactions of preschool children who had recently experienced divorce.[4] They found that the disruption caused by a recent divorce has a substantial effect on the children's play and on their ability to get along with their peers. This effect may be important later in the child's life: unsatisfactory relations with peers can have long-term negative effects on adolescent and adult social and emotional development.

To find out how children play after a divorce, Hetherington and her co-workers watched the children in the classroom and on the playground. Again, boys were more affected than girls, and there were marked changes over time in the children's peer relationships. At two months after divorce, boys and girls showed much less imagination in their play than children from intact families. "They are less able to free themselves from reality. They need a stick to be a sword or a chair to be a castle. They rarely fantasize completely imaginary objects or people. They also show less reversibility in play. Once a stick is a sword, it is not subsequently transformed into a magic wand or a horse."[5] This deficit in imaginative play may be important for the child's social and cognitive development. According to Jerome Singer, an expert on fantasy and play,

> Imaginative play can be viewed as a major resource by which children can cope immediately with the cognitive, affective and social demands of growing up. It is more than a reactive behavior, however, for it provides a practice ground for organizing new schema and for transforming and storing material for more effective later expression in plans, actions, or verbalization.[5]

Not only do children of divorce show less imaginative play; they also do less playing and more watching than children from intact families.

There were marked changes over time in how children of divorce managed with their classmates. By one year after the divorce, the only difference remaining for girls was that the girls from divorced families still showed lowered scores for imaginative play. Two years after the divorce, when the children were six years old, this difference had disappeared. In contrast, boys from divorced families still differed in their play patterns even after two years. They continued to play alone more and showed less cooperative, constructive, imaginative, or game play than boys from intact families. They still watched more than they participated in play. When they did play with other children, they played with younger children and girls rather than with boys of their own age. And they appeared to enjoy playing less: boys from divorced homes were more physically aggressive in the first year and were still less happy and more anxious two years after the divorce. By the end of two years, these boys showed low physical and high verbal aggression—a pattern most commonly seen in girls and which may have resulted from their choice of girls and younger peers as playmates. Their aggressive displays tended to be immature, unprovoked, and ineffective.

Not surprisingly, boys their own age did not respond favorably to these boys of divorced parents. In the first year, their peers either ignored them or returned their nastiness. Even after two years, boys from divorced families were still ignored more and more often isolated by their peers. Few boys from single-parent families were selected as best friends by other boys; they were popular only among younger peers or girls. Girls whose parents are divorced fare better and are generally accepted by their peers after two years. These boys from divorced families have as tough a time coping with peers as they have with their mothers at home. As I will discuss below, however, boys whose fathers stay involved with their children—even though they are not in the home—seem to adjust better at home with their mothers and on the playground with their peers.

DIVORCE AND DEVELOPMENTAL STATUS OF CHILDREN

Hetherington studied children who were 4 years old when their parents were divorced. Are similar effects present at other ages? Divorce is traumatic for children of all ages, but children at different developmental stages have different levels of comprehension and different strategies for coping with the changes surrounding divorce. Preschoolers tend to blame themselves for the divorce: "Daddy left home because I was a bad boy — I didn't put away my toys that day." And they do not understand their parents' emotions, needs, and behavior. Since young children have only poorly formed concepts of families, they often are uncertain about new living arrangements or new patterns of contact between themselves and the departing parent. This often leads to excessive fears of being abandoned and exaggerated hopes of reconciliation.

Children who are older at the time of divorce react differently. Seven- or eight-year-old children are less likely to blame themselves, but fears of abandonment and rejection remain and their interpersonal understanding is still limited. Only by adolescence are children able to understand the divorce process fully, to assign responsibility for the divorce, to resolve loyalty conflicts, and to cope with the economic and social changes that often accompany divorce.

Judith Wallerstein and Joan Kelly, in a study of 60 divorcing families in California, found that preschoolers had the most difficulty in adjusting to the divorce, while adolescents were able to adjust to the trauma more easily. In part this may be due to the adolescents' greater insight into the divorce process. There may be other reasons too, as Hetherington points out: "If the home situation is particularly painful adolescents, more than younger children, do have the option to disengage and seek gratification elsewhere such as in the neighborhood, peer group or school."[7]

FATHER'S ROLE WHEN MOTHER HAS CUSTODY

Even when the mother has custody of the children, the father remains important. Hetherington found that, at first, many divorced fathers had almost as much face-to-face contact with their children as fathers in intact homes — a reminder that many fathers in nondivorced families do not spend much time with their children. At two months after the divorce, the fathers' influence was still evident. However, fathers in this study were generally less available as time passed. After two years, the fathers had much less contact with their children than they had had immediately after the divorce. Of the 48 fathers in the study, 19 fathers saw their children once a week, 21 fathers saw them every 2 or 3 weeks, and 8 once a month or less.

Other investigators report similar patterns of a gradual decline in father-child contact after divorce. In her study of 560 divorced parents, in which nearly 90 percent of the mothers had sole custody of the children, Julie Fulton found that in only one-fifth of the families was there a steady pattern of visitation in the two years after divorce by the noncustodial parent — usually the father.[8] In 50 percent there was a decline in visitation, and in 28 percent of the families, the noncustodial parent never visited.

It is not simply indifference or lack of interest on the part of the fathers that accounts for these visitation patterns. The custodial parent's attitude is important too. Fulton found that nearly 40 percent of the wives with custody had refused to permit their ex-husbands to see the children at least once — and the children's health, safety, or wishes had nothing to do with the refusal. As Fulton notes, "Custodial parents are attempting to make a new life for themselves and their children and many of their decisions and actions serve to keep the other parent at a distance.[9]

In her study Hetherington found that as the father's amount of contact declined, so did his influence. Furthermore, the fathers' impact on their children's behavior declined while that of the mothers increased. In intact families, mothers' behavior is generally less important in sex-typing than fathers' behavior, but in divorced families, the mother's influence becomes much more important. Single mothers are more influential in teaching their children — especially their sons — what types of behavior are considered appropriate for their sex. Many divorced mothers raise sons who by traditional standards are highly masculine; they do it by encouraging traditionally masculine sex-typed behaviors — independence and exploration — and by maintaining a positive attitude toward their former husbands. However, as Hetherington and her colleagues note:

> Many mothers in single parent families are overprotective, infantalizing, and erractically restrictive with their sons. They are apprehensive when their children indulge in adventurous or boisterous activities . . . in combination with viewing a father as undesirable, these maternal activities may mediate the timorous, dependent behaviors and feminine sex-role typing sometimes found in some of the boys in single parent families.[10]

This decline in the father's influence and accompanying rise in the mother's impact on children's sex-typing is not inevitable when the mother has custody. The fathers in Hetherington's study who maintained frequent contact with their children over the two-year period following divorce had children who were more stereotypically sex-typed. In other words, by sustaining a regular and continuing relationship with their children, divorced fathers can continue to affect their children's social and emotional development.

Departures from the traditional masculine and feminine stereotypes are, of course, not necessarily problematic; in fact many would view these shifts toward more androgynous sex roles for boys and girls as positive and beneficial. The particular combinations of sex-typed behaviors that boys and girls are likely to exhibit — whether in divorced or intact families — depend on the kinds of role models that parents provide, and the behaviors that they encourage and value in their children.

The amount of contact between divorced fathers and their

children varies widely across families, and even may depend on the sex of the child. Robert Hess and Kathleen Camara found that boys saw their fathers more frequently and for longer periods than girls did and were more often in touch with their fathers between visits.[11] In view of the greater difficulty that the boys in the Hetherington study experienced after divorce, it is possible that fathers see their sons more often in an attempt to alleviate some of the problems — a reminder of the bidirectionality of influence among family members. Or maybe fathers place special value on their relationship with their sons — a preference, as we saw in Chapter 3, that is evident even in fathers' earliest interactions with their newborn babies.

Hess and Camara describe the wide range of patterns of contact that they observed in their families:

> Some fathers saw their children every week and talked with them on the phone often. Others visited them infrequently and visits were not predictable. For some, the father's residence was a second home. Visits were for long weekends, holidays or other periods that gave the children the opportunity to become, for a short time, a part of the father's life and household. The children were given responsibilities around the house, not treated as guests. Another pattern was one in which the father picked up the children on an afternoon on the weekend, took them to the park, then to a restaurant, then delivered them to their homes — the "Disneyland father," as two of the parents in our study called it. The routine of the house — preparing meals, fixing items around the home and yard, mowing the lawn, repairing bikes, and such — were not occasions for interaction for these fathers. While the contact between father and children may have been cordial, the children were kept at a distance from the father's new life.[12]

As I have stressed throughout this book, fathers can affect their children both directly and indirectly though their relationship with other family members. This is clearly seen in divorced fathers who affect their children not only though direct interaction but also indirectly by the support they give the mother in her parenting role. Hetherington and her colleagues found that the mother's effectiveness in dealing with the child was related to support from her ex-husband in childrearing and agreement with her ex-husband in disciplining the child. When divorced couples agreed with and supported each other, the disruption in family functioning appeared to be less extreme and the restabilizing of family functioning occurred earlier — by the end of the first year as opposed to two years.

The effects of father contact are not short-lived. Wallerstein and Kelly found that even five years after divorce

> the most crucial factor influencing a good readjustment was a stable, loving relationship with *both* parents between whom friction had largely dissipated, leaving regular dependable visiting patterns that the parent with custody encouraged . . . The contribution that the out of home parent could make emerged with clarity at five years. Frequent, flexible visiting patterns remained important to the majority of children.

Nearly one-quarter of the children in this study continued to see their fathers weekly, while another 20 percent saw their fathers two to three times a month. The 17 percent who saw their fathers less than once a month continued to be anguished by their fathers' inattentiveness; even after five years these children still wished for more contact with their fathers. Overall, Wallerstein and Kelly "found that 30 percent of the children had an emotionally nurturant relationship with their fathers five years after the marital separation and that this sense of a continuing close relationship was critical to the good adjustment of both boys and girls." These investigators explain it this way: "The father's presence kept the child from a worrisome concern with abandonment and total rejection and from the nagging self-doubts that follow such worry. The father's presence, however limited, also diminished the child's vulnerability and aloneness and total dependency on one parent."[13]

Contact between a father and his children following divorce is not always helpful, however. In some cases such contact can be harmful. According to Hetherington, when a divorced father disagrees with his former wife about childrearing, when he has negative attitudes toward her, and when he is emotionally immature, it is better that he have little contact with the family. In this case, frequent visits by the father are associated with poor relations between mother and child and with disruptions in the child's behavior. Wallerstein and Kelly confirm these observations. They found that almost one-fifth of the children in such situations did not find the visits pleasurable or gratifying. A number resented being used to carry hostile messages between parents. As one 13-year-old put it, "My father has to understand that when he shoots arrows at my mother, they first have to go through our bodies before they reach her."[14] The father who visits erratically can cause his child to feel "rejected, rebuffed, and unloved and unloveable."

The message of these studies is clear: quality of contact between fathers and their children is more important than the amount of contact. As Hess and Camara concluded: "The child's confidence in the tie with the father apparently depended less on frequency of scheduling than it did on the quality of interaction that took place when they did meet."[15]

It is important to remember that the best situation for children of divorce is one in which close relationships with both parents are maintained — not just with the father *or* the mother. A good relationship with one parent helps, but keeping close ties to both mother and father is even better. Hess and Camara compared three groups of children of divorce: children who had positive relationships with both parents, children who had negative relationships with both, children who had a positive relationship with one parent and a negative relationship with the other. These three patterns of relationship had strikingly different impacts on children. Those who maintained positive relationships with both parents had the lowest scores on measures of stress and aggression and were rated more highly on work effectiveness and social interaction with peers. Where both relationships were unsatisfactory, the negative effects of divorce were most severe. However, recall from Chapter 4 that Mary Main found that for infants a good relationship with one parent could compensate, at least in part, for a poor relationship with the other parent. Hess and Camara found a similar effect among their children of divorced families. The children who had a positive relationship with one parent were nearly identical to children who had good relationships with both parents on measures of aggression and stress and were between the groups of children who had either positive or negative relationships with both parents in their work effectiveness and their ability to get along with their peers. Clearly, relationships with *both* parents need to be considered. Unfortunately Hess and Camara did not investigate whether the mother-child or father-child relationship is more important or, more critically, whether it is better for the child to have a positive relationship with the parent who has custody. A situation in which a child lives with one parent but wishes to be with the other obviously is not ideal. Unraveling the complexities of the impact of divorce on families has only begun.

PATERNAL CUSTODY

Sometimes fathers gain custody following divorce and children are raised in a home with a father as the single caregiver. What effect does this reversal of the usual child-care arrangement have on the child? Although we tend to take maternal custody in divorce cases for granted, it is a twentieth-century phenomenon. Before this century, under English law, children (and wives) were viewed as property of the husband, and fathers were nearly always granted custody of their children. A father had to be grossly unfit before an exception was made. In 1817, for example, the poet Shelley was denied custody of his children on the grounds of his "vicious and immoral" atheistic beliefs. In our century, by contrast, until very recently fathers were typically awarded custody only if the mother was viewed as exceptionally incompetent.

The view that mothers are uniquely suited — both biologically and psychologically — to raise children has prevailed. And this attitude is generally held by the courts, who "have long paid lip service to a 'best interest' doctrine when child custody is at issue, but in practice, courts have been guided by the generalization that the

mother should be awarded custody except in extreme circumstances."[16] In the 1970s the situation has shifted, and the inevita-
bility of maternal custody is being challenged. Consider this
legal opinion from a judge of the New York Family Court:

> The simple fact of being a mother does not by itself indicate a ca-
> pacity or willingness to render a quality of care different from
> that which the father can provide. The traditional and romantic
> view, at least since the turn of the century, has been that nothing
> can be an adequate substitute for mother love . . . Later decisions
> have recognized that this view is inconsistent with informed ap-
> plication of the best interests of the child doctrine and out of
> touch with contemporary thought about child development and
> male and female stereotypes.[17]

At the same time that our conceptions of sex roles for mothers
and fathers are changing and father's competence as a parent and
caretaker is being documented and recognized, more fathers are
seeking custody of their children. Similarly, as more women join
the workforce, some women are questioning their allegiance to
the mothering role; women are seeking custody of their children
somewhat less often. As a result of both these trends, fathers are
winning custody more often. As indicated earlier, in 1979, approximately 10 percent of divorced fathers had custody of their
children in the United States and about 7 percent in Great Britain.

Since paternal custody is a new and still relatively rare phenomenon, our understanding of its effects is limited. The results
from the handful of studies that are available are consistent and
help to set aside some myths and prejudices. Who are the divorced men who receive custody of their children? To find out,
Kelin Gersick studied 40 recently divorced fathers, half of whom
were awarded custody of their children and half of whom were
not. Contrary to popular expectations, the men who sought and
gained custody were not a younger, more radical group with unusual life styles. Instead, they were older, more established, and
in a higher socioeconomic position. Possibly they could afford
better legal aid, and perhaps they were viewed more favorably
by the judges. And these men were not more likely to come from

divorced homes; there were no differences between the custody and noncustody fathers in the percentages of disrupted and intact families of origin. Interestingly, the men who had custody of their children had more intense relationships with their own mothers and more distance from their fathers than did the men who did not have custody, who were close to both parents. The mothers of the fathers who had custody generally had assumed more complete responsibility for child care and had not worked outside the home. These men may have patterned themselves after their mothers, who provided a child-oriented model of parenting. As one father who had custody put it: "I guess I'm more similar to my mother. We certainly share an interest in child rearing". The intriguing aspect of this pattern, in Gersick's words, is that "men from traditional families are more likely to make the extremely nontraditional decision to seek custody."[18]

In spite of their increasing numbers, fathers with custody of their children are still viewed as "brave explorers of the new sex role frontier."[19] Consequently people often treat them differently from the way they treat divorced mothers who have custody. Fathers with custody receive more offers of help, say in the form of babysitting or dinner invitations. And they generally get more credit: "Isn't George a terrific father and he does it alone!" How often do single mothers get extra credit for managing on their own? For fathers, raising children singlehandedly is considered a special role, while for single mothers, it's expected that they should and can do it.

Men who do gain custody generally manage the tasks of child care effectively. Fathers with custody are not bumbling and ineffectual characters who can't change a diaper, fry an egg, or vacuum a carpet. Divorced fathers can raise their children competently and effectively. And recent research supports this claim. Helen Mendes asked single fathers, the majority of whom had received custody following divorce, how they coped with the daily chores of homemaking: "Twenty-eight of the thirty-two fathers regularly cooked, cleaned, shopped, and managed their homes. None of the fathers acknowledged that he had any feeling of lack of masculinity because he had to perform these functions. Most of the fathers knew how to cook prior to becoming single fathers."[20] Although many single fathers — just like single mothers — experience considerable stress as they try to coordinate the multiple tasks of caring for the home and the children, they do master these new tasks.

How do fathers with custody affect their children's development? As we saw in the Hetherington project, boys do not fare as well as girls following divorce — at least when mother has custody. The question arises as to whether boys and girls show the same pattern of adjustment when father has custody. Or does a different pattern emerge, with boys in paternal custody showing less disruption than girls? John Santrock and Richard Warshak recently investigated the impact of maternal versus paternal custody on the social development of boys and girls.[21] Their results suggest that children who live with the opposite-sex parent are less well-adjusted than children living with the same-sex parent. Their conclusion is based on a careful evaluation of how fathers and mothers with custody relate to their 6-to-11-year-old children in a problem-solving task in the laboratory. The families were videotaped while parent and child planned an activity together and discussed the main problems of the family. Based on these videotaped observations, Santrock and Warshak found a variety of differences in the children — depending on the custody arrangement. For boys, paternal custody appeared to be beneficial: the boys who lived with their fathers were more mature and more sociable and displayed higher levels of self-esteem than boys who were in their mother's custody. For girls, the opposite was the case: they were less demanding, more independent, and more mature when in the custody of their mothers.

A similar picture emerges from ratings that were made when the children were interviewed. Girls who lived with their father were seen as less cooperative and less honest than girls in their mother's custody. Similarly, the boys in paternal custody were more honest and more cooperative than the boys in maternal custody. These findings suggest that paternal custody may be a better arrangement for boys — but not for girls — when a divorce does occur. Santrock and Warshak note the implication of their findings:

There appears to be something drastically important about the ongoing, continuous relationship of a child with the same-sex parent. For example, when fathers are given the major role in rearing both boys and girls, they may sense what the psychologically healthy needs of boys are more so than girls. Similarly, when mothers are given virtually sole responsibility for rearing their children, as in a mother custody divorce arrangement, they too may bring to the situation a better sense of girls' needs more so than boys.[22]

However, we need to be careful in interpreting Santrock and Warshak's findings or in generalizing from their sample of fathers to all divorced fathers. As I pointed out earlier, men who do receive custody may be unusual in some ways, since the awarding of custody to fathers is still uncommon. These fathers may have been unusually talented and devoted parents, or possibly they had already developed particularly close relations with their children—which may have been one reason for awarding them custody in the first place.

Children in paternal and maternal custody have different kinds of lives and experiences. Fathers tend to use additional caretakers, such as the mother, babysitters, relatives, day care centers, and friends more than do mothers. More specifically, children in paternal custody see their mothers more often than children in maternal custody see their fathers. Children whose fathers have custody also are enrolled in day care for more hours a week (24 hours versus 11 hours).

Whether fathers seek those social supports more often or whether friends, relatives, and neighbors just feel that fathers need more help than mothers in rearing their children has not been determined. Since men are typically perceived as less capable caregivers than women—research evidence aside—it would not be surprising if fathers who raise children by themselves received more unsolicited help. These social support systems appear to be important: regardless of the type of custody, the total amount of contact with additional adult caretakers is directly linked to the child's warmth, sociability, and social conformity, at least as they show up in the laboratory. It is less clear why these social supports are beneficial. Perhaps they enable children to receive more and higher-quality adult involvement both from the additional caretakers and from the parent they live with, whose resources are less depleted. Possibly, children in general benefit from contact with a richer and expanded social network of people who can offer additional support as well as alternative role models. Fathers, mothers, and children are best understood when their ties to people and institutions outside the family are considered.

Regardless of the custody arrangements, fathers themselves may learn from the experience of caring for their children that may result following a divorce. Kristine Rosenthal and Harry Keshet, who recently studied 129 separated or divorced men, suggest that "men who have separated from or divorced their wives and have taken on some major responsibility for their children's care find that the demands of that responsibility can become an important focus for their own growth." Moreover, they conclude that children not only need their fathers, but "men need their children . . . In learning to take care of his children's needs, a man learns to take care of his own."[23]

FATHER AS STEPPARENT

Another role is emerging for men as a result of the increasing number of divorces — the role of stepfather. Often excluded from custody of their own children, many men assume routine responsibilities for other children through remarriage. In 1978, 10 percent of children in the United States lived with one natural parent and one stepparent, and the stepparent was usually a father. Demographers predict that by 1990 15 percent of U.S. children will be living with a stepparent.

How successfully children accept a stepfather depends on the children's age. In her study of more than 21,000 remarriages Jessie Bernard found that very young children and postadolescent children tend to accept a stepparent more easily than adolescents. Henry Biller and Dennis Meredith explain this phenomenon: "Becoming a stepfather to a teenager is particularly difficult. The young person has already done a lot a maturing emotionally and has established his ties elsewhere. He is also fighting for his own independence from the family and is not in a position to establish close ties with a new family member."[24]

Even with younger children, the arrival of a stepfather can create tensions in the family — especially in the early stages. One of the main problems, according to Judith Wallerstein and Joan Kelly, is timing: "only a few men appeared sensitive to the need to cultivate a relationship with stepchildren gradually and to make due allowance for suspiciousness and resistance in the initial stages." Instead, Wallerstein and Kelly found, most of the stepfathers moved too quickly into the parent role and assumed "the prerogatives and authority that this position traditionally conveys."[25] In spite of difficult beginnings, however, these investigators found that the relationships between the preadolescent children and their stepfathers became "happy and gratifying to both child and adult."

One of the tough problems that children face when their mother remarries is how to maintain relationships with two fathers — their biological father and their stepfather. Wallerstein and Kelly investigated this issue as well. Contrary to some expectations, they found that in happily remarried families children do not experience serious problems or conflicts, nor do biological fathers fade out of their children's lives. A great many of the fathers in their study continued to visit their children after their ex-wives remarried, much as they had earlier. And the children accommodated by enlarging their view of the family to make room for three parents — mother, father, and stepfather. As ten-year-old Jerry said when asked how often he saw his father, "Which Dad do you mean?"

Wallerstein and Kelly did find some problems in families of remarriage:

> The most tragic situations for the child were those in which mother and stepfather demanded that the child renounce his or her love for the father as the price for acceptance and affection within the remarried family. Such children were severely troubled

and depressed, too preoccupied with the chronic unresolvable conflict to learn to develop at a normal pace.[26]

Thus it is important that the mother and stepfather allow and even encourage the child's love for the biological father. If neither father nor stepfather tries to monopolize the children's affection, the children have room in their lives for close relationships with both their fathers — and both fathers can help the children develop.

What are the long-term effects on children of growing up in a home with a stepfather? Are children better off living with just one parent, or does remarriage benefit the children? Of course the answers to these questions vary from family to family. As for overall trends, the evidence is mixed. Some investigators report that the presence of a stepfather has beneficial effects — especially for teaching boys the behaviors traditionally considered masculine. Others are not so positive about the impact of "reconstituted" families and argue that "remarriage and the presence of a stepfather tend to create more problems than they solve."[27] In a national survey of children, Nicholas Zill found that children living with mothers and stepfathers were significantly more likely to be seen as "needing help" than were children in mother-father or single-parent homes.[28] Clearly, divorce and the subsequent adjustments that children must make are difficult and remarriage may bring new problems and require even further new adjustments. However, parents and stepparents who are sensitive to the child's needs can develop good family relationships. The case is far from closed, and no easy recipe is available to ensure that remarriage will be the answer for children of divorce.

IS DIVORCE NECESSARILY NEGATIVE?

Divorce tends to be disruptive, stressful, and painful for mothers and fathers as well as for children. I have noted many of the negative effects on children's behavior that often follow divorce. But divorce may be the best alternative for some families. Many researchers have found that children in single-parent families are better off than children in conflict-ridden intact families. Separation from one parent does not have to have bad effects. Eventual escape from the conflict of an unhappy unbroken home may be a positive outcome of divorce for children. In some families, then, divorce is a well-considered action by a couple to end tension, anguish, and discord. In the words of Margaret Mead, "Every time we emphasize the importance of a happy secure home for children, we are emphasizing the rightfulness of ending marriages when homes become unhappy and insecure."

7 / Innovations in Fathering

Divorced fathers with custody are not the only fathers who are caring for their children these days. The traditional division of labor between father and mother is being challenged and changed in many two-parent families. Some social changes, such as paternity leaves, shorter work weeks, and flexible working hours, allow men more time to be with their children. In families where both mother and father work outside the home, the father often shares more in child care. In some families the traditional economic roles are reversed: the mother goes off to work each day and the father is the homemaker. What do these innovative ways of organizing the family mean for children?

TIME FOR FATHERING

In most industrialized countries it is usual for a woman to take some time off from her job—some maternity leave—after she delivers her baby. What about leave for fathers? Paternity leave gives a father a chance to learn about and to enjoy his new baby from the beginning. Instead of a brief visit at feeding time and a glance through the nursery window—all on a lunch hour or after a full day on the job—leaves for fathers permit a more leisurely introduction to fatherhood. Paternity leave is gaining acceptance slowly in the United States; in some other countries it is already common. In Sweden, for example, recent government legislation allows all men a period of paid leave from their usual work schedule after their infant is born. Recent evidence suggests that more than 60 percent of Swedish fathers take some advantage of these opportunities, although only about 15 percent take a month or more of paid leave during their babies' first year. As Maureen Green notes, "an allotted span of time for a young father to be around the house and enjoy the first weeks of his son's or daughter's life is beginning to be thought of less as an eccentricity, and more as a personal necessity."[1] Whether this chance to get to know the new baby alters the father's later relationship with his child is still untested, but it seems a likely possibility.

Flexible working hours may also give men more time for fathering. Flexible hours, for example, may permit fathers to stay home later in the morning and get their children ready for school; or alternatively, to be at home to greet the children after their day at school. Relationships between children and their fathers might be very different if fathers were available for these daily child-care routines. Recent evidence from Scandinavian countries, such as reports from the Volvo factory in Sweden, indicates that flexible working hours are economically feasible and may have positive benefits for both families and employers. But other evidence suggests that flex-time may not make much difference in family relations. In a recent study of 700 people in two U.S. government agencies, of which one agency was on flex-time and the other on a regular schedule, Halcy Bohen and Anemaria Viveros-Long asked how workers in both agencies allocated their time between work and home.[2] Neither mothers nor fathers who were on flex-time reported spending more time with their children than did workers on regular schedules. However, people on flex-time generally reported less conflict between their home and work responsibilities than those on regular schedules. Perhaps, the quality of the relationship between parent and child may improve—even if the amount of time does not shift. It is clear that merely making more time available to parents does not guarantee that the time will be devoted to children. As James Levine points out:

> Free time won't and can't be used by all men or women to attend
> to their children; there is shopping, community, and church

work, bowling and so forth. In many cases, free time will mean a second job in order to meet family expenses in an inflationary economy. What's important here, however, is not only the possibility for new relationships, but recognition of the fact that men too have a family stake in job restructuring."[3]

Other changes in the work world are offering even greater possibilities for men to share in the care and rearing of their children. Although most men still hold full-time jobs, "part time work for full time parents," in Levine's phrase, is becoming more common in both the United States and Europe. One type of part-time work arrangement is the split job, whereby a husband and wife share the same job, but each person works only part time. On some U.S. college campuses, for example, some recent Ph.D.'s have shared a single faculty position. In Norway Erik Gronseth studied 16 couples who either shared a single job or both held part-time jobs, and found that most were motivated to try this arrangement by a desire for better relationships with their children. In these families, most of whom had pre-schoolers, mother and father shared equally in child care but the wife still did most of the housework. Many aspects of family life improved as a result of these shifts in work and child care responsibilities. Fathers reported that they had "better and more open contact" with their children, felt closer to them, and understood them better. Mothers benefited too, and enjoyed their children more — because of their reprieve from full-time child care. Nearly everyone in the study thought that "the children are the ones whose interests are best served by the work sharing pattern."[4]

However, the marital relationship of these work-sharing couples improved as well. Couples reported less conflict, improved solidarity, and more mutual understanding. This effect may have been good for the children too, of course, since the way the parents feel about each other can influence their relationships with the children. Recall from Chapter 3 that Frank Pedersen showed that the husband-wife relationship influenced how effectively the mother fed her baby. In summary, Gronseth found that the work-sharing families experienced "less strain and stress and better marital and parent-child relations than they did prior to the adoption of the pattern."[5] This way of organizing work and family life is likely to remain rare, but its advantages for both parents and children may make it attractive to more couples in the future, especially during the years when their children are small.

The shorter work week is another innovation that may affect relationships between fathers and children. Do fathers who work longer days but fewer days spend more time with their families? David Maklan compared men who worked four ten-hour days a week with men who worked five eight-hour days.[6] The men who worked four days a week devoted nearly four more hours a week to child care, but there were no differences in the amount of time devoted to housework. Possibly men do want to spend time with their children but do not usually have the chance to do so — but evidently they have no similar craving to do housework. The father's assumption of a larger share of child-care tasks may improve his relationship with his children and may also, by relieving the mother of some of the routine of child care, make her relationship with the children more enjoyable as well. It is not yet clear just how giving fathers more uninterrupted time at home affects their children. It is apparent, however, that this reorganization of work schedules does allow more contact between father and child. Thus it appears to be a promising way to "make time for fathering."

THE DUAL CAREER FAMILY

More mothers are working outside the home today than at any earlier time in our history. The number of working mothers has increased rapidly in most industrialized nations. One recent estimate indicates that 35 percent of women in the United States with children under 3 years of age are working. The percentage of women in the workforce rises rapidly as children grow older. In the United States nearly 60 percent of mothers are in the marketplace rather than at home by the time their children are 6 years old.

What does this situation mean for fathers? Do fathers take more responsibility for child care or simply persist in their traditional pattern when mothers work outside the home? Recent studies in the United States and Australia suggest that fathers, in general, change their ways when mother is employed too. In his book *How Americans Use Time*, John Robinson reports that husbands of women who are employed full time are more involved in child care than husbands of women who are not employed or work only part time. Graeme Russell found similar trends in Australian families. When both parents were employed, fathers doubled their contribution to child care, but mothers still carried most of the burden of routine caretaking.[7] Role sharing increases when mother and father both work, but women are still doing the major part of the diaper detail.

Even though fathers do less than half the work of child care, their participation can have a positive effect on both the working mother and the child. Michael Lamb and Susan Bronson explain it this way: "By assuming partial responsibility for home and/or child care, such a husband relieves his wife of some of her responsibilities, freeing her time for more unhurried interaction with the child . . . The husband's participation has a beneficial impact on the mother-child relationship and so affects the child's development indirectly." When fathers persist in their traditional ways and refuse to participate, Lamb and Bronson continue, both mother and child may suffer:

When her husband fails to assume significant domestic responsibilities, the working mother has little time available for unhurried interaction with the child since there are multiple compelling demands on her time. The child of such a mother can clearly be deemed "at risk." Neither of its parents are able or willing to commit much time to it and the interaction that it has with its mother is hurried, insensitive, and dominated by routine activities like feeding and bathing. Father, meanwhile, is not consistently sensitive to the child's needs because he does not define this as within his province.[8]

ROLE-SHARING FAMILIES

Many mothers work outside the home, but fathers who assume an equal role in child care are still rare. Even less common are fathers who reverse roles with mothers and become full-time caregivers to their children. In spite of their rarity, families in which mothers and fathers have radically departed from traditional roles are well worth examining. They can tell us a good deal about the possible roles that fathers can play in the family and the possible ways in which families can reorganize themselves to provide more flexibility for both parents and children.

Graeme Russell studied 50 Australian families in which fathers took major or equal responsibility for child care.[9] In these families, fathers and mothers shared about equally (55 percent for mothers, 45 percent for fathers) the full range of child-care tasks such as feeding, diapering, and bathing. In traditional families, by comparison, fathers performed these tasks only about 12 percent of the time.

More time was devoted to play in nontraditional families — mostly because fathers were interacting more with their children. Just as in traditional families, nontraditional fathers play more than mothers, while mothers spend more time reading to the children and helping with schoolwork. As we saw in earlier chapters, fathers and mothers in traditional families tend to have different styles of play, with fathers being more physical and engaging in more outdoor games. When fathers share caregiving, however, play styles change: the stereotyped roles of father as football coach and mother as storyteller are less evident in these families. In some of Russell's role-sharing families both mothers and fathers engaged in both indoor and outdoor activities; in others fathers spent more time talking, singing, and drawing with their children than roughhousing or playing football. Recall from Chapter 3 that this same kind of shift in style of play begins in infancy. Fathers who are full-time caregivers for their young babies show some of the same play styles as full-time mothers.

These nontraditional role-sharing families have different attitudes toward sex roles than conventional families. Not surprisingly, fewer of the role-sharing fathers feel that a mother's place is in the home. And the parents in nontraditional families have greater faith in the father's ability to care for children. More than 80 percent of the fathers and 90 percent of the mothers in nontraditional families believed that fathers could be capable caregivers—although some felt that fathers were still not as good as mothers. In contrast, only 49 percent of the fathers and 65 percent of the mothers in the traditional families felt that fathers were capable of taking care of children. Why do parents decide to adopt this family arrangement—to have mother be the breadwinner and father the homemaker? While some parents reported that they simply believed that they should share the care of their children, a majority of families adopted this life-style for economic reasons. Interestingly, the reasons for adopting this life-style and the reasons for continuing it may be different. As one father put it:

> We started out doing it because of money . . . we wanted to buy a house. When we got the house, Barbara wanted to stop working . . . she wanted me to go back to a 9 to 5 job. I didn't want to because that would have meant that I wouldn't have seen the kids as much. I felt I had as much right to see the kids as she did. The way we were meant we both take care of them for about equal time. I want it to stay like that.

There are distinct benefits for both mothers and fathers from sharing or switching roles. Mothers report increased self-esteem as a result of the opportunity to return to work. As one mother said, "After going back to work I started to value myself more . . . I have also become more pleasant." And fathers benefit too. Fathers who take care of their children report that their relationships with the children improved: "I think it has increased the amount of pleasure I get from them." "Being with them all the time has helped cement my relationship with them." "I became a lot more involved, understood her a lot better, and got on a lot better with her."

The parents in Russell's study did not believe that the children suffered as a result of this unorthodox family arrangement. According to one father, "There doesn't seem to be any bad side of it from Luke's [the child's] point of view. He has adjusted well."[10]

There is information on just how having their father as primary caretaker does affect children, and the father in Russell's study was right. There do not seem to be any negative effects, and there are apparently some positive effects for both parents and children. In the United States, Norma Radin studied families with preschool children in which the father was the primary caregiver. These fathers were responsible for their preschooler about 60 percent of the time; in comparison; traditional fathers in Radin's study cared for their children only 22 percent of the time.[11] What kinds of men take on the nontraditional role of caregiver? The traditional and nontraditional fathers did not differ in terms of their own self-reported masculinity; men who were raising their children were just as masculine, assertive, and forceful as men whose wives were primarily responsible for childcare. Both traditional and nontraditional fathers in this study had grown up in homes with traditional fathers. However, both mothers and fathers who chose this nontraditional arrangement came from homes with working mothers—a pattern that may have helped to set the style for their choice of family organization. The wives in the nontraditional families had enjoyed their interaction with their own fathers, even though their fathers had been relatively uninvolved in childrearing.

When fathers were primary caretakers both boys and girls showed greater internality—a higher belief in their own ability to control their fate and to determine what happens to them—than did children in traditional families. As noted in Chapter 5, this belief in one's ability to control external events is important for children's later achievement. Radin suggests that "creators of new roles particularly in defiance of social norms would perceive themselves as masters of the major outcomes in their lives"[12] and, in turn, would provide models of self-determination for their developing children.

While boys usually profit from their father's involvement more than girls, in the case of the highly involved fathers, Radin found that daughters benefited as well. Both boys and girls who were primarily raised by their fathers scored higher on verbal ability than the children raised in traditional families in this study. Child-rearing fathers set higher educational and career expectations for their sons *and* their daughters than traditional fathers. And these highly involved fathers worked harder at producing their future doctors and lawyers by stimulating their children's cognitive growth more. Girls, in particular, benefited, and the childrearing fathers try hardest with their daughters "perhaps to combat sexist influences they will experience in the larger society."[13] However, while fathers in these nontraditional families increase their efforts to stimulate children, mothers in these families provide less stimulation than mothers in traditional families. Thus the children receive a different combination of parental stimulation.

Some areas of development were unaffected by these role reversals. The preschoolers' sex-role identification is unaffected by this type of family structure. Not surprisingly, however, some of their sex-role expectations about who takes on household duties are altered. When asked who generally uses common household objects, such as a dishwasher or a vacuum cleaner, children give less stereotyped answers in the families where dad is the primary caretaker.

Parents who reverse roles are a very recent phenomenon, and evidence suggesting that children from these families fare better is not conclusive. Such parents may be different in other ways from parents who maintain traditional roles, and might have influenced their children differently from "traditional" parents, no matter which parent stayed home with the children. However, it is likely that parents who reverse roles are significantly affected by their choice, and that therefore the nontraditional environment in which their children develop is at least partially responsible for differences between children from traditional and nontraditional families. As new family role arrangements become more common and more intensively studied, the effects of role reversal and other innovations will be better understood.

It seems that few couples persist in sharing child care. In a sobering follow-up investigation two years after his first Australian study, Graeme Russell found that only about one-fourth of his role-sharing families were continuing with this arrangement.[14] A number of factors may account for the small number of families that choose these alternatives and persist in them. For example, in general men are still paid more than women, so that most families may find that it makes better economic sense for the father to be the breadwinner. Men may be reluctant even to request leaves of absence that may jeopardize their job security — particularly in times of scarce jobs and inflation. In some cases, such as when the mother is breastfeeding a child, these role reversals may be difficult to implement. The basic problem, however, may still be one of attitude; as James Levine points out: "There is still the widespread belief that a man does not belong at home taking care of children."[15] Until there is some change in this traditional view about the roles that men and women can or should play in rearing their children, few families will either try alternative patterns or persist in them for extended periods of time.

SOCIETAL SUPPORT FOR FATHERING

While girls have opportunities and encouragement to learn "how to mother" as they grow up, boys receive little clear information about how to be fathers. As one researcher puts it,

> Almost nothing in the prefatherhood learning of most males is oriented in any way to training them for this role. Males are actively discouraged as children from play activities involving baby surrogates, and, except in rare instances of large families with few or no older sisters, they are not usually required to help much in the daily care of young siblings. In short, a new father has only the vaguest idea of what he is expected to do and how he ought to do it.[16]

We need to give future fathers opportunities to acquire and

practice fathering skills. Fortunately, neither fathers nor mothers exist in a social vacuum. As I have stressed throughout this book, families should be viewed as existing within a wider social network of relatives, friends, neighbors, and institutions. These individuals and groups that are outside the immediate family can play an important part in supporting fathers and in helping them become wise and effective parents.

As early as 1925, the PTA advocated that education for parenthood begin during adolescence, in high school. Today there are many programs across the United States aimed at preparing girls and boys for the day when they will become parents. In these programs future fathers and mothers learn about such subjects as child development and basic child-care skills, as well as the economics of raising a family and the impact of children on a couple's social life. For the adolescent boys who take them, such courses provide an opportunity to acquire caretaking skills and realistic expectations about fatherhood. Few boys sign up for these classes, however. To many boys and young men, fatherhood seems too remote to worry about.

Interest in parenthood, as we saw in Chapter 2, increases during pregnancy, and men get another chance to learn if they accompany their wives to childbirth preparation classes. However, in one assessment of the effect of Lamaze childbirth classes, "many men said they were pleased with their training for childbirth, but felt totally unprepared for what comes after."[17] These classes do well at what they intend to accomplish — preparing fathers and mothers for the experience of childbirth; but they focus little on postpartum caretaking skills.

A better time to teach fathering may be immediately after birth during the mother's postpartum hospital stay, when the father may be both accesible and highly motivated to learn parenting skills. Recent evidence from studies in Sweden and the United States suggests that men can learn a great deal about fathering during this period. In Sweden, John Lind let fathers feed their infants, undress them, and change their diapers while they were still in the hospital. This chance to learn was effective:

these fathers were more involved in infant care and household tasks three months later than fathers who had not cared for their infants in the hospital.[18]

My colleagues and I recenty tried a somewhat similar experiment in the United States.[19] We showed fathers a videotape on fathering soon after their babies' birth, while mother and baby were still in the hospital. The videotape provided information about the newborn infant's perceptual and social competence, about play techniques, and about caretaking skills. Then we observed fathers who had watched the videotape and fathers who had not seen the videotape while they fed and played with their infants. We also questioned them about their attitudes toward childcare and their knowledge about infant development, and three months later we checked how often they fed and diapered their babies at home. The men who had viewed the videotape knew more about infant perceptual capacities, were more responsive to their infants during feeding and play; and fed and diapered their babies more often at three months than fathers who had not seen the videotape. However, the videotape increased the fathers' involvement only if their babies were boys; fathers of girls were unaffected. This selective effect is similar to earlier findings that fathers are more involved with sons than with daughters.

Learning to be an active and involved father need not be restricted to this early period just after the baby is born. Men can learn fathering skills at a variety of times. Furthermore, different men need support at different times. Some fathers may be good at the early chores of feeding and diapering, but be at a loss for how to play with their active 2-year-old. Others will do just fine when their kids are old enough for math problems and football, but will have difficulty with those early feedings in the middle of the night. In the case of parents who adopt their children, learning to parent may begin when the child is three months old or three years. There is no clear evidence that the period right after birth is in any sense a "critical" time for men to learn fathering skills or to develop an emotional tie to their infants.

To further illustrate that fathers (and mothers) can learn new skills, consider a recent study by Jane Dickie and Sharon Carna-han.[20] They selected 19 families who were interested in learning more about their 4- to 11-month-old infants. Ten families — mothers and fathers — attended eight weekly classes that taught them how to read and respond to infant signals appropriately and that focused on differences in infant temperament. The remaining nine families received no training. To assess the effects of the training, the investigators observed mother, father, and infant in the home. The training had its greatest impact on the fathers, who increased their interactions with their infants, while the mothers who participated in the training sessions decreased their interactions with their babies. Perhaps as fathers' competence increases, mothers are more willing to relinquish some of the childrearing tasks to their spouses. In fact, these "trained" parents — both mothers and fathers — were rated overall as more competent than the untrained parents, and not just by the observers: trained mothers and fathers thought their spouses were more competent than did untrained parents. In contrast to the untrained fathers, the trained fathers touched, held, and looked at their infants more and were more likely to smile and talk in response to the baby's behavior. And the infants seemed to appreciate their trained parents' new skills: they sought to interact most with the trained fathers and least with the untrained fathers. Mothers were selected by their infants for play and interaction more in the untrained families than in the trained families — in part, because the fathers in trained families were receiving a large share of the infants' attention. The infants benefited from the training too — and were rated as more responsive than infants of families who did not receive training.

In another recent study, Philip Zelazo and his colleagues showed that fathering skills can be improved even in families where fathers do very little playing or caretaking.[21] They selected 20 fathers with year-old sons and "tutored" 12 of these fathers by demonstrating a variety of games, toys, and play strategies that could be used with their infants. After the tutoring, the fathers played with their infants for half an hour each day for four weeks at home. The other 8 fathers received no tutoring.

The infants whose fathers had learned and practiced new play-ing skills showed more interest in their fathers than the infants whose fathers had not been tutored. In addition, the infants of the tutored fathers looked at their dads more often and initiated play more frequently. Thus improving fathers' interaction skills seemed to make the relationship between father and infant closer.

Together these intervention efforts suggest that fathering skills can be learned and that this learning can take place at a variety of times in the father's life. Learning to father effectively is a con-tinuing process as the child's development requires new skills on the part of the parent to meet the child's changing needs. At pres-ent, we have only begun to explore the ways that fathers (and mothers) can be aided in this task.

There is no "average" father. Family organization and sex roles are changing rapidly in our society, and the definition of father-ing is no longer rigid or restricted. Many of the facts reported in this book come from studies of traditional families, in which the father is the breadwinner and the mother cares for the children. But I have also presented evidence from families that are part of society's transition — families in which fathers share in child care or even reverse roles with their wives, and families in which fa-ther or mother is a single parent. This book is a progress report of what we know today about how fathers act and how they in-fluence their children.

One thing is clear: fathers are perfectly capable of caring for children, even very young babies. They are not simply substi-tute mothers; mothers and fathers have distinct styles of parent-ing. Fathers tend to spend more of their available time playing with their children than mothers do, and to play differently. Their physical and robust approach complements and contrasts with mothers' verbal, paced style. Children profit from this di-versity of experience. These patterns are not fixed, however, and they are likely to evolve as social and work roles for men and women continue to change.

Fathers and families do not exist in isolation. They are embedded in wider communities and cultures, and the support they get from friends, relatives, neighbors, and institutions is important. I have mentioned ways that society can adjust the demands of work, for example, to make fathering more possible and more enjoyable. Institutions, too, such as hospitals and schools, can help fathers learn to be effective parents and can provide advice and assistance when families have problems.

Fathers are no longer, if they ever were, merely a biological necessity — a social accident. They are an important influence on their children's development. And a close relationship between father and child benefits the father as well as the child. Children need their fathers, but fathers need their children, too.

References
Suggested Reading
Index

References

1 *Fatherhood: Myths and Realities*

1. R. R. Sears, E. E. Maccoby, and H. Levin, *Patterns of Child Rearing* (Evanston, Ill. Row, Peterson, 1956); J. M. W. Whiting and I. L. Child, *Child Training and Personality* (New Haven: Yale University Press, 1953).
2. M. Ribble, *Rights of Infants* (New York: Columbia University Press, 1943); R. A. Spitz, "Hospitalism: An Inquiry into the Genesis of Psychiatric Conditions in Childhood," *Psychoanalytic Study of the Child*, 1945, *1*, 53-74. For a review of these early studies see L. J. Yarrow, "Separation from Parents during Early Childhood," in M. L. Hoffman and L. W. Hoffman, eds., *Review of Child Development Research*, I (New York: Russell Sage Foundation, 1964).
3. J. Bowlby, *Maternal Care and Mental Health* (Geneva: World Health Organization, 1951); J. Bowlby, *Attachment and Loss*, I *Attachment* (New York: Basic Books, 1969).
4. D. B. Lynn, *The Father: His Role in Child Development* (Monterey: Brooks Cole, 1974).
5. M. M. West and M. J. Konner, The Role of the Father: An Anthropological Perspective," in M. Lamb, ed., *The Role of the Father in Child Development* (New York: Wiley, 1976).
6. I. DeVore, "Mother-Infant Relations in Free Ranging Baboons," in H. L. Rheingold, ed., *Maternal Behavior in Mammals* (New York: Wiley, 1963).
7. A. Chamove, H. J. Harlow, and G. D. Mitchell, "Sex Differences in the Infant-Directed Behavior of Preadolescent Rhesus Monkeys," *Child Development*, 1967, *38*, 329-335.
8. G. D. Mitchell, "Paternalistic Behavior in Primates," *Psychological Bulletin*, 1969, *71*, 399-417; G. D. Mitchell, W. K. Redican, and J. Gomber, "Males Can Raise Babies," *Psychology Today*, 1974, *7*, 63-67; W. K. Redican, "Adult Male–Infant Interactions in Non-Human Primates," in Lamb, ed., *The Role of the Father in Child Development*; R. D. Parke and S. J. Suomi, "Adult Male–Infant Relationships: Human and Nonhuman Primate Evidence," in K. Immelman, G. Barlow, M. Main, and L. Petrinovitch, eds., *Behavioral Development: The Bielefeld Interdisciplinary Project* (New York: Cambridge University Press, in press).

9. J. S. Rosenblatt, "The Development of Maternal Responsiveness in the Rat," *American Journal of Orthopsychiatry*, 1969, *39*, 36-56.

10. M. Kotelchuck, "The Infant's Relationship to the Father: Experimental Evidence," in Lamb, ed., *The Role of the Father in Child Development*.

11. M. P. M. Richards, J. F. Dunn, and B. Antonis, "Caretaking in the First Year of Life: The Role of Fathers and Mothers' Social Isolation," *Child: Care, Health and Development*, 1977, *3*, 23-26.

12. A. Szalai, ed., *The Use of Time: Daily Activities of Urban and Suburban Populations in Twelve Countries* (The Hague: Mouton, 1972).

13. See L. W. Hoffman, "Effects of Maternal Employment on the Child — A Review of the Research," *Developmental Psychology*, 1974, *10*, 204-228.

14. F. A. Pedersen, B. J. Anderson, and R. L. Cain, "An Approach to Understanding Linkages between the Parent-Infant and Spouse Relationships" (paper presented at the Society for Research in Child Development, New Orleans, March 1977).

15. Ibid.

16. See U. Bronfenbrenner, *The Ecology of Human Development* (Cambridge: Harvard University Press, 1979).

17. M. Green, *Fathering* (New York: McGraw-Hill, 1976).

2 The Expectant Father

1. P. M. Shereshefsky and L. J. Yarrow, *Psychological Aspects of a First Pregnancy and Early Postnatal Adaptation* (New York: Raven Press, 1973).

2. D. R. Entwisle and S. G. Doering, *The First Birth* (Baltimore: Johns Hopkins University Press, forthcoming).

3. S. J. Bittman and S. R. Zalk, *Expectant Fathers* (New York: Hawthorn Books, 1978).

4. J. Cain, "The Couvade or 'Hatching,' " *The Indian Antiquary*, 1874, *3*, 151, cited in J. H. Wapner, "An Empirical Approach to the Attitudes, Feelings and Behaviors of Expectant Fathers" (Ph.D. diss., Northwestern University, 1975).

5. W. H. Trethowan and M. F. Conolon, "The Couvade Syndrome," *British Journal of Psychiatry*, 1965, *111*, 57-66; B. Liebenberg, "Expectant Fathers," *American Journal of Orthopsychiatry*, 1967, *37*, 358-359; B. Liebenberg, "Expectant Fathers," *Child and Family*, 1969 *8*, 265-277.

6. Bittman and Zalk, *Expectant Fathers.*

7. Entwisle and Doering, *The First Birth.*

8. W. Masters and V. Johnson, *Human Sexual Response* (Boston: Little, Brown, 1966).

9. H. L. Rausch, W. A. Barry, R. K. Hertel, and M. A. Swain, *Communication, Conflict and Marriage* (San Francisco: Jossey Bass, 1974).

10. J. D. Gladieux, "Pregnancy — The Transition to Parenthood: Satisfaction with the Pregnancy Experience as a Function of Sex-Role Conceptions, Marital Relationship and Social Network," in W. B. Miller and L. F. Newman, eds., *The First Child and Family Formation* (Chapel Hill, N.C.: Carolina Population Center, 1978).

11. Ibid., p. 292.

12. Bittman and Zalk, *Expectant Fathers*, p. 166.

13. F. K. Grossman et. al., *Pregnancy, Birth, and Parenthood* (San Francisco: Jossey Bass, 1980).

14. Entwisle and Doering, *The First Birth.*

15. C. Legg, I. Sherick, and W. Wadland, "Reaction of Preschool Children to the Birth of a Sibling," *Child Psychiatry and Human Development,* 1974, *5,* 3-39.

16. A. L. Baldwin, "Changes in Parent Behavior during Pregnancy: An Experiment in Longitudinal Analysis," *Child Development,* 1947, *18,* 29-39.

17. C. R. Phillips and J. T. Anzalone, *Fathering: Participation in Labor and Birth* (St. Louis: Mosby, 1978).

18. Ibid., pp. 46-47.

19. R. Fein, "Men's Experiences before and after the Birth of a First Child" (Ph.D. diss., Harvard University, 1974).

20. W. J. Hennenborn and R. Cogan, "The Effect of Husband Participation on Reported Pain and the Probability of Medication during Labor and Birth," *Journal of Psychosomatic Research,* 1975, *19,* 215-222.

21. Entwisle and Doering, *The First Birth.*

22. Ibid.

23. Ibid.

24. M. Levine and R. Block, unpublished study, cited by J. C. McCullagh, *Baby Talk,* June 1980, p. 3.

25. M. Gainer and P. Van Bonn, "Two Factors Affecting the Caesarean Section Delivered Mother: Father's Presence at the Delivery and Postpartum Teaching" (Master's thesis, University of Michigan School of Nursing, 1977).

26. F. A. Pedersen, M. T. Zaslow, R. L. Cain, and B. J. Anderson, "Caesarean Birth: The Importance of a Family Perspective" (paper presented at the International Conference on Infant Studies, New Haven, Conn., April 1980).

27. J. Lind, "Observations after Delivery of Communications between Mother-Infant-Father" (paper presented at the International Congress of Pediatrics, Buenos Aires, October 1974).

3   Fathers and Infants

1. M. Greenberg and N. Morris, "Engrossment: The Newborn's Impact upon the Father," *American Journal of Orthopsychiatry*, 1974, *44*, 526.

2. R. D. Parke and S. E. O'Leary, "Father-Mother-Infant Interaction in the Newborn Period: Some Findings, Some Observations and Some Unresolved Issues," in K. Riegel and J. Meacham, eds., *The Developing Individual in a Changing World*, II, *Social and Environmental Issues* (The Hague: Mouton, 1976).

3. D. Phillips and R. D. Parke, "Father and Mother Speech to Prelinguistic Infants" (unpublished manuscript, University of Illinois, 1979).

4. J. Sachs, "The Adaptive Significance of Linguistic Input to Prelinguistic Infants," in C. E. Snow and C. A. Ferguson, eds., *Talking to Children* (Cambridge: Cambridge University Press, 1977).

5. S. L. Bem, "The Measurement of Psychological Androgyny," *Journal of Consulting and Clinical Psychology*, 1974, *42*, 155-162.

6. S. S. Feldman and S. C. Nash, "Sex Differences in Responsiveness to Babies among Mature Adults," *Developmental Psychology*, 1979, *15*, 430-436.

7. A. M. Frodi, M. E. Lamb, L. A. Leavitt, and W. L. Donovan, "Fathers' and Mothers' Responses to Infant Smiles and Cries," *Infant Behavior and Development*, 1978, *1*, 197.

8. A. M. Frodi, M. E. Lamb, L. A. Leavitt, W. L. Donovan, C. Neff and D. Sherry, "Fathers' and Mothers' Responses to the Faces and Cries of Normal and Premature Infants," *Developmental Psychology*, 1978, *14*, 490-498.

9. P. H. Wolff, "The Natural History of Crying and Other Vocalizations in Early Infancy," in B. Foss, ed., *Determinants of Infant Behavior*, IV (London: Methuen, 1969); O. Wasz-Hockert, J. Lind, V. Vuorenkoski, T. Partanen, and E. Valanne, *The Infant Cry: A Spectographic and Auditory Analysis* (Suffolk: Lavenham Press, 1968).

10. R. D. Parke and D. B. Sawin, "Infant Characteristics and Behavior as Elicitors of Maternal and Paternal Responsivity in the Newborn Period." (paper presented at the Biennial meeting of the Society for Research in Child Development, Denver, April 1975); R. D. Parke and D. B. Sawin, "The Father's Role in Infancy: A Re-evaluation," *The Family Co-ordinator*, 1976, *25*, 365-371.

11. R. D. Parke and D. B. Sawin, "The Family in Early Infancy: Social Interactional and Attitudinal Analyses," in F. A. Pedersen, ed., *The Father-Infant Relationship: Observational Studies in the Family Setting* (New York: Praeger, 1980).

12. C. P. Cowan, P. A. Cowan, L. Coie, and J. D. Coie, "Becoming a Family: The Impact of a First Child's Birth on the Couple's Relationship," in W. B. Miller and L. F. Newman, eds., *The First Child and Family Formation* (Chapel Hill, N.C.: Carolina Population Center, 1978).

13. M. Kotelchuck, "The Infant's Relationship to the Father: Experimental Evidence," in M. E. Lamb, ed., *The Role of the Father in Child Development* (New York: Wiley, 1976); M. P. M. Richards, J. F. Dunn, and B. Antonis, "Caretaking in the First Year of Life: The Role of Fathers, and Mothers' Social Isolation" *Child: Care, Health and Development*, 1977, *3*, 23-26.

14. J. T. Hawthorne, M. P. M. Richards, and M. Callon. "A Study of Parental Visiting of Babies in a Special Care Unit," in F. S. W. Brimble-combe, M. P. M. Richards, and N. R. C. Roberton, eds., *Early Separation and Special Care Nurseries* (London: Simp/Heinemann Medical Books, 1978); M. W. Yogman, "Development of the Father-Infant Relationship," in H. Fitzgerald, B. Lester, and M. W. Yogman, eds., *Theory and Research in Behavioral Pediatrics*, vol. I (New York: Plenum Press, forthcoming).

15. J. V. Brown and R. Bakeman, "Relationships of Human Mothers with Their Infants during the First Year of Life: Effects of Prematurity," in R. W. Bell and W. P. Smotherman, eds., *Maternal Influences and Early Behavior* (Holliswood, N.Y.: Spectrum, 1980). S. Goldberg, "Premature Birth: Consequences for the Parent-Infant Relationship," *American Scientist*, 1979, *67*, 214-220.

16. K. Minde, S. Trehub, C. Corter, C. Boukydis, B. Celhoffer, and P. Marton, "Mother-Child Relationships in the Premature Nursery: An Observational Study" (unpublished manuscript, Department of Psychiatry, The Hospital for Sick Children, Toronto, Canada, 1977).

17. G. Russell, "The Father Role and Its Relation to Masculinity, Femininity and Androgyny," *Child Development*, 1978, *49*, 1174-1181.

18. Parke and Sawin, "Infant Characteristics and Behavior as Elicitors of Maternal and Paternal Responsivity"; Parke and Sawin, "The Father's Role in Infancy."

19. G. Russell, "Fathers as Caregivers: Possible Antecedents and Consequences" (paper presented to a study group on Fathers and Social Policy, University of Haifa, Israel, July 15-17, 1980).

20. F. A. Pedersen, R. Cain, M. Zaslow, and B. Anderson, "Variation in Infant Experience Associated with Alternative Family Organization" (paper presented at the International Conference on Infant Studies, New Haven, Conn., April 1980); D. Entwisle and S. Doering, *The First Birth* (Baltimore: Johns Hopkins University Press, forthcoming).

21. R. Schaffer, *Mothering* (Cambridge: Harvard University Press, 1977), p. 37.

22. Kotelchuck, "The Infant's Relationship to the Father."

23. Richards, Dunn, and Antonis, "Caretaking in the First Year of Life;" M. E. Lamb, "Father-Infant and Mother-Infant Interaction in the First Year of Life," *Child Development*, 1977, *48*, 167-181.

24. Pedersen, Cain, Zaslow, and Anderson, "Variation in Infant Experience Associated with Alternative Family Role Organization."

25. M. Yogman, S. Dixon, E. Tronick, H. Als, and T. B. Brazelton, "The Goals and Structure of Face-to-Face Interaction between Infants and Fathers" (paper presented at the Biennial Meeting of the Society for Research in Child Development, New Orleans, March 1977).

26. T. B. Brazelton, "Behavioral Competence of the Newborn Infant," *Seminars in Perinatology*, 1979, *3*, 42.

27. J. Bruner, "Early Social Interaction and Language Acquisition," in H. R. Schaffer, ed., *Studies in Mother-Infant Interaction* (London: Academic Press, 1977).

28. T. G. Power and R. D. Parke, "Play as a Context for Early Learning: Lab and Home Analyses," in I. E. Sigel and L. M. Laosa, eds., *The Family as a Learning Environment* (New York: Plenum, in press).

29. See Lamb, "Father-Infant and Mother-Infant Interaction"; M. E. Lamb, "The Development of Mother-Infant and Father-Infant Attachments in the Second Year of Life," *Developmental Psychology*, 1977, *13*, 637-649; and M. Lamb, "The Father's Role in the Infant's

Social World," in J. H. Stevens and M. Mathews, eds., *Mother-Child, Father-Child Relationships* (Washington, D.C.: National Association for the Education of Young Children, 1978; K. A. Clarke-Stewart, "The Father's Contribution to Children's Cognitive and Social Development in Early Childhood," in Pedersen, ed., *The Father-Infant Relationship*.

30. T. Field; "Interaction Behaviors of Primary versus Secondary Caretaker Fathers," *Developmental Psychology*, 1978, *14*, 183-185.

31. Pedersen, Cain, Zaslow, and Anderson, "Variation in Infant Experience Associated with Alternative Family Organization."

32. Clarke-Stewart, "The Father's Contribution to Children's Cognitive and Social Development"; A. Clarke-Stewart, "And Daddy Makes Three: The Father's Impact on Mother and Young Child," *Child Development*, 1978, *49*, 466-478; D. B. Lynn and A. R. Cross, "Parent Preference of Preschool Children," *Journal of Marriage and the Family*, 1974, *36*, 555-559.

33. L. W. Hoffman, "Changes in Family Roles, Socialization, and Sex Differences," *American Psychologist*, 1977, *32*, 644-658.

34. Parke and O'Leary, "Father-Mother-Infant Interaction in the Newborn Period"; Parke and Sawin, "Infant Characteristics and Behavior as Elicitors of Maternal and Paternal Responsivity"; E. B. Thoman, P. H. Leiderman, and J. P. Olson, "Neonate-Mother Interaction during Breast Feeding," *Developmental Psychology*, 1972, *6*, 110-118; E. B. Thoman, C. Barnett, and P. H. Leiderman, "Feeding Behaviors of Newborn Infants as a Function of Parity of the Mother," *Child Development*, 1971, *42*, 1471-1483.

35. R. D. Parke and D. B. Sawin, "The Family in Early Infancy."

36. Kotelchuck, "The Infant's Relationship to the Father"; Power and Parke, "Play as a Context for Early Learning."

37. J. Rubin, F. J. Provenzano, and Z. Luria, "The Eye of the Beholder: Parents' Views on Sex of Newborns," *American Journal of Orthopsychiatry*, 1974, *43*, 720-731.

38. H. B. Gewirtz and J. L. Gewirtz, "Visiting and Caretaking Patterns for Kibbutz Infants: Age and Sex Trends," *American Journal of Orthopsychiatry*, 1968, *38*, 427-443; M. M. West and M. J. Konner, "The Role of the Father: An Anthropological Perspective," in Lamb, ed., *The Role of the Father in Child Development*.

39. W. K. Redican, "Adult Male-Infant Interactions in Nonhuman Primates," in Lamb, ed., *The Role of the Father in Child Development*, pp. 345-385.

4 *Socialization and Sociability*

1. R. Schaffer, *Mothering* (Cambridge: Harvard University Press, 1977), p. 98.
2. A. Macfarlane, "Olfaction in the Development of Social Preferences in the Human Neonate," in *Parent-Infant Interaction* (Amsterdam: CIBA Foundation Symposium 33, new series, Associated Scientific Publishers, 1975).
3. H. R. Schaffer and P. E. Emerson, "The Development of Social Attachments in Infancy," *Monographs of the Society for Research in Child Development*, 1964, *29*, no. 3 (serial no. 94).
4. F. A. Pedersen and K. S. Robson, "Father Participation in Infancy," *American Journal of Orthopsychiatry*, 1969, *39*, 466-472.
5. M. Kotelchuck, "The Infant's Relationship to the Father: Experimental Evidence," in M. E. Lamb, ed., *The Role of the Father in Child Development* (New York: Wiley, 1976).
6. M. E. Lamb, "Father-Infant and Mother-Infant Interaction in the First Year of Life," *Child Development*, 1977, *48*, 167-181.
7. See R. D. Parke, "Parent-Infant Interaction: Progress, Paradigms and Problems," in G. P. Sackett, ed., *Observing Behavior*, I, *Theory and Applications in Mental Retardation* (Baltimore: University Park Press, 1978).
8. E. Rendina and J. D. Dickerscheid, "Father Involvement with First-Born Infants," *Family Coordinator*, 1976, *25*, 373-379; A. M. Frodi, M. E. Lamb, M. Frodi, C. P. Hwang, B. Forsstrom, and T. Corry; "Stability and Change in Parental Attitudes Following an Infant's Birth into Traditional and Nontraditional Swedish Families" (unpublished manuscript, University of Michigan, 1980).
9. F. A. Pedersen, J. Rubinstein, and L. J. Yarrow, "Infant Development in Father-Absent Families," *Journal of Genetic Psychology*, 1979, *135*, 51-61.
10. K. A. Clarke-Stewart, "The Father's Contribution to Children's Cognitive and Social Development in Early Childhood," in F. A. Pedersen, ed., *The Father-Infant Relationship: Observational Studies in the Family Setting* (New York: Praeger, 1980).
11. M. Main and D. R. Weston, "The Independence of Infant-Mother and Infant-Father Attachment Relationships: Security of Attachment Characterizes Relationships, not Infants." (unpublished manuscript, University of California, Berkeley, 1980).

12. For a general discussion of this issue see M. D. Ainsworth, "The Development of Infant-Mother Attachment," in B. M. Caldwell and H. N. Ricciuti, eds., *Review of Child Development Research*, III (Chicago: University of Chicago Press, 1973).

13. E. Waters, J. Wippman, and L. A. Sroufe, "Attachment, Positive Affect, and Competence in the Peer Group: Two Studies in Construct Validation," *Child Development*, 1979, 50, 821-829.

14. L. M. Stolz, *Father Relations of War-Born Children: The Effect of Postwar Adjustment of Fathers on the Behavior and Personality of First Children Born While the Fathers were at War* (Stanford: Stanford University Press, 1954); D. B. Lynn and W. L. Sawrey, "The Effects of Father Absence on Norwegian Boys and Girls," *Journal of Abnormal and Social Psychology*, 1959, 59, 258-262.

15. E. M. Hetherington, "Effects of Paternal Absence on Sex-Typed Behaviors in Negro and White Preadolescent Males," *Journal of Personality and Social Psychology*, 1966, 4, 87-91.

16. B. Biller, *Paternal Deprivation* (Lexington, Mass.: D. C. Heath, 1974); E. M. Hetherington and J. Deur, "The Effects of Father Absence on Child Development," in W. W. Hartup, ed., *The Young Child*, II (Washington, D.C.: National Association for the Education of Young Children, 1972).

17. J. W. Santrock, "Relation of Type and Onset of Father-Absence on Cognitive Development," *Child Development*, 1972, 43, 455-469.

18. M. M. Johnson, "Sex Role Learning in the Nuclear Family," *Child Development*, 1963, 34, 315-333; E. M. Hetherington, "Effects of Father Absence on Personality Development in Adolescent Daughters," *Developmental Psychology*, 1972, 7, 313-326.

19. F. A. Pedersen, "Does Research on Children Reared in Father-Absent Families Yield Information on Father Influence?," *The Family Coordinator*, 1976, 25, 459-464.

20. E. M. Hetherington, "A Developmental Study of the Effects of Sex of the Dominant Parent on Sex Role Preference, Identification and Imitation in Children," *Journal of Personality and Social Psychology*, 1965, 2, 188-194.

21. S. F. Fisher, *The Female Orgasm: Psychology, Physiology, Fantasy* (New York: Basic Books, 1973).

22. J. H. Langlois and A. C. Downs, "Mothers, Fathers, and Peers as Socialization Agents of Sex-Typed Play Behaviors in Young Children," *Child Development*, 1980, 51, 1217-1247.

23. R. D. Parke and D. B. Sawin, "Children's Privacy in the Home: De-

128 / References

velopmental, Ecological, and Child-Rearing Determinants," *Environment and Behavior*, 1979, *11*, 87-104.

5 *Intellectual Development*

1. L. J. Yarrow, J. L. Rubinstein, and F. A. Pedersen, *Infant and Environment: Early Cognitive and Motivational Development* (New York: Halsted Press, 1975), p. 86.

2. C. S. Dweck, "Achievement," in M. E. Lamb, ed., *Social and Personality Development* (New York: Holt, Rinehart and Winston, 1978).

3. F. A. Pedersen, J. L. Rubinstein, and L. J. Yarrow, "Infant Development in Father-Absent Families," *Journal of Genetic Psychology*, 1979, *135*, 51-61.

4. Ibid., p. 60.

5. K. A. Clarke-Stewart, "And Daddy Makes Three: The Father's Impact on Mother and Young Child," *Child Development*, 1978, *49*, 466-478; and K. A. Clarke-Stewart, "The Father's Contribution to Children's Cognitive and Social Development in Early Childhood," in F. A. Pedersen, ed., *The Father-Infant Relationship: Observational Studies in the Family Setting* (New York: Praeger Publishers, 1980).

6. B. L. White, B. Kaban, B. Shapiro, and J. Attonucci, "Competence and Experience," in I. C. Uzgiris and F. Weizmann, eds., *The Structuring of Experience* (New York: Plenum Press, 1976), pp. 150-151.

7. L. W. Hoffman, "Changes in Family Roles, Socialization, and Sex Differences," *American Psychologist*, 1977, *32*, 649.

8. R. W. Blanchard and H. B. Biller, "Father Availability and Academic Performance among Third Grade Boys," *Developmental Psychology*, 1971, *4*, 301-305; H. B. Biller, *Father, Child and Sex Role* (Lexington, Mass.: D. C. Heath, 1971), p. 59.

9. M. Shinn, "Father Absence and Children's Cognitive Development," *Psychological Bulletin*, 1978, *85*, 295-324.

10. P. H. Leiderman and G. F. Leiderman, "Familial Infant Development in an East African Agricultural Community," in E. J. Anthony and C. Koupernik, eds., *The Child in His Family: Children at Psychiatric Risk*, III (New York: John Wiley and Sons, 1974); R. B. Zajonc, "Family Configuration and Intelligence," *Science*, 1976, *192*, 227-236.

11. N. Radin, "The Role of the Father in Cognitive, Academic, and Intellectual Development," in M. E. Lamb, ed., *The Role of the Father in Child Development* (New York: Wiley, 1976).

12. M. P. Honzik, "Environmental Correlates of Mental Growth: Prediction from the Family Setting at Twelve Months," *Child Development*, 1967, *38*, 337-364; N. Radin, "The Role of the Father in Cognitive, Academic, and Intellectual Development," p. 259.
13. J. H. Block, "Another Look at Sex Differentiation in the Socialization Behaviors of Mothers and Fathers," in *Psychology of Women: Future Directions of Research* (New York: Psychological Dimensions, 1979), p. 25.
14. Hoffman, "Changes in Family Roles."
15. Radin, "The Role of the Father," p. 253.
16. M. C. Rau, *Indira Priyadarshini* (New Delhi: Popular Book Services, 1966), cited in M. L. Hamilton, *Father's Influence on Children* (Chicago: Nelson-Hall, 1977), p. 33.
17. M. Mead, *Blackberry Winter* (New York: Morrow, 1972), pp. 40, 41, 44.

6 Divorce and Custody

1. E. M. Hetherington, "Divorce: A Child's Perspective," *American Psychologist*, 1979, *34*, p. 851.
2. E. M. Hetherington, M. Cox, and R. Cox, "The Aftermath of Divorce," in J. H. Stevens, Jr., and M. Mathews, eds., *Mother-Child, Father-Child Relations* (Washington, D.C.: National Association for the Education of Young Children, 1978.)
3. Ibid., pp. 163, 170.
4. E. M. Hetherington, M. Cox, and R. Cox, "Play and Social Interaction in Children Following Divorce," *Journal of Social Issues*, 1979, *35*, 26-49.
5. Ibid., p. 38.
6. J. L. Singer, "Television, Imaginative Play and Cognitive Development: Some Problems and Possibilities" (paper presented at the meeting of the American Psychological Association, San Francisco, Sept. 1977), p. 10.
7. J. S. Wallerstein and J. B. Kelly, *Surviving the Break-up: How Children Actually Cope with Divorce* (New York: Basic Books, 1980); Hetherington, "Divorce: A Child's Perspective," p. 853.
8. J. A. Fulton, "Parental Reports of Children's Post-Divorce Adjustment," *Journal of Social Issues*, 1979, *35*, 126-139.
9. Ibid, p. 134.
10. E. M. Hetherington, M. Cox and R. Cox, "Family Interaction and the Social, Emotional, and Cognitive Development of Children Following Divorce," in V. Vaughn and T. B. Brazelton, eds., *The Fam-

ily: Setting Priorities (New York: Science and Medicine, 1979), p. 20.

11. R. D. Hess and K. A. Camara, "Post-Divorce Relationships as Mediating Factors in the Consequences of Divorce for Children," *Journal of Social Issues*, 1979, *35*, 79-96.

12. Ibid., 93-94.

13. J. S. Wallerstein and J. B. Kelly, "California's Children of Divorce," *Psychology Today*, 1980, *13*, 71-72.

14. Ibid., 71.

15. Hess and Camara, "Post-Divorce Relationships as Mediating Factors," p. 94.

16. J. W. Santrock and R. Warshak, "Father Custody and Social Development in Boys and Girls," *Journal of Social Issues*, 1979, *35*, 113.

17. Cited in J. A. Levine, *Who Will Raise the Children: New Options for Fathers (and Mothers)* (New York: Lippincott, 1976), p. 45.

18. K. E. Gersick, "Fathers by Choice: Divorced Men Who Receive Custody of Their Children," in G. Levinger and O. C. Moles, eds., *Divorce and Separation* (New York: Basic Books, 1979), p. 320.

19. Levine, *Who Will Raise the Children*, p. 48.

20. H. A. Mendes, "Single Fathers," *The Family Coordinator*, 1976, *25*, 439-444.

21. Santrock and Warshak, "Father Custody and Social Development."

22. Ibid., pp. 116-117.

23. K. M. Rosenthal and H. F. Keshet, *Fathers without Partners: A Study of Fathers and the Family after Marital Separation* (Totowa, N.J.: Rowman and Littlefield, 1980).

24. J. Bernard, *Remarriage: A Study of Marriage* (New York: Dryden Press, 1956); H. B. Biller and D. L. Meredith, *Father Power* (New York: David McKay, 1974), p. 292.

25. Wallerstein and Kelly, "California's Children of Divorce," p. 74.

26. Ibid., p. 76.

27. C. Longfellow, "Divorce in Context: Its Impact on Children," in Levinger and Moles, eds., *Divorce and Separation*, p. 289.

28. N. Zill, "Divorce, Marital Happiness, and the Mental Health of Children: Findings from the Foundation for Child Development National Survey of Children" (paper prepared for National Institute of Mental Health Workshop on Divorce and Children, Bethesda, Md., 1978).

7 *Innovations in Fathering*

1. M. Green, *Fathering* (New York: McGraw-Hill, 1976), p. 216

2. H. Bohen and A. Viveros-Long, *Balancing Jobs and Family Life: Do Flexible Work Schedules Help?* (Philadelphia: Temple University Press, 1981).

3. J. A. Levine, *Who Will Raise the Children: New Options for Fathers (and Mothers)* (New York: Lippincott, 1976), p. 91.

4. E. Gronseth, "Work-Sharing: Adaptations of Pioneering Families with Husband and Wife in Part-Time Employment," *Acta Sociologia*, 1975, *18*, 218.

5. Ibid., p. 219

6. D. Maklan, "The Four Day Workweek: Blue-Collar Adjustment to a Nonconventional Arrangement of Work and Leisure Time" (Ph.D. diss., University of Michigan, 1976), cited in J. P. Robinson, *How Americans Use Time* (New York: Praeger, 1977).

7. Robinson, *How Americans Use Time*; G. Russell, "Fathers as Caregivers: Possible Antecedents and Consequences" (paper presented to a study group on The Role of the Father in Child Development, Social Policy, and the Law, University of Haifa, Israel, July 15-17, 1980).

8. M. E. Lamb and S. K. Bronson, "The Role of the Father in Child Development: Past Presumptions, Present Realities, and the Future Potential" (paper presented to a conference on Fatherhood and the Male Single Parent, Omaha, Neb., Nov. 1978).

9. Russell, "Fathers as Caregivers."

10. Ibid.

11. N. Radin, "Childrearing Fathers in Intact Families: An Exploration of Some Antecedents and Consequences" (paper presented to a study group on The Role of the Father in Child Development, Social Policy, and the Law, University of Haifa, Israel, July 15-17, 1980).

12. N. Radin, "Childrearing Fathers in Intact Families with Preschoolers" (paper presented at the annual meeting of the American Psychological Association, Toronto, Sept. 1978), p. 12.

13. Ibid., p. 23.

14. Russell, "Fathers as Caregivers."

15. Levine, *Who Will Raise the Children*, p. 153.

16. J. S. Chafetz, *Masculine, Feminine or Human* (Itasca, Ill.: F. E. Peacock, 1978), p. 197.

17. A. S. Wente and S. Crockenberg, "Transition to Fatherhood: Lamaze Preparation, Adjustment Difficulty and the Husband-Wife Relationship," *The Family Coordinator*, 1976, *25*, p. 356.

18. R. Lind, "Observations after Delivery of Communications between

Mother-Infant-Father" (paper presented at the International Congress of Pediatrics, Buenos Aires, October 1974).

19. R. D. Parke, S. Hymel, T. G. Power, and B. R. Tinsley, "Fathers and Risk: A Hospital Based Model of Intervention," in D. B. Sawin, R. C. Hawkins, L. O. Walker, and J. H. Penticuff, eds., *Psychosocial Risks in Infant-Environment Transactions*, (New York: Bruner/Mazel, 1980).

20. J. Dickie and S. Carnahan Gerber, "Training in Social Competence: The Effect on Mothers, Fathers, and Infants," *Child Development*, 1980, *51*, 1248-1251.

21. P. R. Zelazo, M. Koetlehuck, L. Barber, and J. David, "Fathers and Sons: An Experimental Facilitation of Attachment Behaviors" (paper presented at the Biennial Meeting of the Society for Research in Child Development, New Orleans, March 1977).

Suggested Reading

Sam Bittman and Sue Rosenberg Zalk, *Expectant Fathers* (New York: Hawthorn Books, 1978). A popular introduction to the father's role in pregnancy, childbirth, and early infancy, written by a professional writer and a clinical psychologist.

Michael E. Lamb, ed., *The Role of the Father in Child Development* (New York: John Wiley and Sons, 1981). The most comprehensive set of integrative reviews of research on fathers available. The volume includes reviews by leading researchers on social and cognitive development in infants and children as well as cross-cultural, historical, and comparative reviews.

James A. Levine, *Who Will Raise the Children? New Options for Fathers (and Mothers)* (Philadelphia: J. B. Lippincott, 1976). One of the pioneering works on alternative roles for fathers. Based on a series of interviews, Levine explores issues such as househusbands, single fathers, and adoptive fathers in a nontechnical style.

David B. Lynn, *The Father: His Role in Child Development* (Belmont, Calif.: Wadsworth Publishing Company, 1974). A fine introduction to the father's role in social and cognitive development.

Frank A. Pedersen, ed., *The Father-Infant Relationship: Observational Studies in the Family Setting* (New York: Praeger Publishers, 1980). An excellent collection of research reports, focusing on observational studies of father-infant and mother-infant interaction with a focus on the family context.

Rhona Rappaport, Robert N. Rappaport, and Ziona Strelitz, *Fathers, Mothers, and Society* (New York: Basic Books, 1977). A comprehensive examination of research relating to issues of parenting across the life span with emphasis on recent changes in roles for mothers and fathers.

Index